D0944960

A Voyage in Vain

other books by Alethea Hayter

A SULTRY MONTH:
Scenes of London Literary Life in 1846

OPIUM AND THE ROMANTIC IMAGINATION

HORATIO'S VERSION

A VOYAGE IN VAIN

Coleridge's Journey to Malta in 1804

ALETHEA HAYTER

FABER AND FABER
3 Queen Square
London

First published in 1973
by Faber and Faber Limited
3 Queen Square London WC1
Printed in Great Britain by
Ebenezer Baylis & Son Ltd
The Trinity Press, Worcester, and London
All rights reserved

ISBN 0 571 10240 9

Contents

Contents

Illustrations

Acknowledgements

The main substance of this book is drawn from Professor Kathleen Coburn's edition of Coleridge's *Notebooks*, and from Professor E. L. Griggs's edition of his *Letters*, and like everyone else who writes about Coleridge today, I owe a vast debt to the learning, insight and diligence of these two scholars. I am very grateful to Messrs Routledge & Kegan Paul and to the Clarendon Press, Oxford, for permission to quote numerous passages from Coleridge's notebooks and letters. The other main source for information about Coleridge's voyage to Malta which I have used is the logs of the two warships escorting the convoy in which he travelled, which are preserved in the Public Record Office. I am also grateful to the following publishers for permission to quote copyright material: the Clarendon Press, Oxford, for *Letters of William and Dorothy Wordsworth*, edited by Ernest de Selincourt; Professor E. L. Griggs for *Coleridge Fille*; G. Bell for *Light and Colour in the Open Air* by M. G. J. Minnaert. A list of these and other sources consulted is given on pages 175–82. Mr Geoffrey Grigson's *The Romantics* and *The Harp of Aeolus* were particularly helpful on the subject of the "Glory".

Mr Oliver Warner, out of his vast knowledge of naval history, gave me invaluable advice, for which I am most grateful, about where to look for information about convoys and the war at sea in 1804. Dr Sanderson, Mr Archibald, and other members of the staff of the National Maritime Museum gave me much help over illustrations. I am grateful to the British Museum, the National Maritime Museum, the Master and Fellows of Jesus College, Cambridge, and the Gibraltar Tourist Office, London, for permission to reproduce paintings, drawings, prints and photographs.

After I had planned this book, Mr Donald Sultana published his

Acknowledgements

Coleridge in Malta and Italy, one chapter of which covers the same ground as this book in some detail; but the main theme of his work is the political situation in the Mediterranean at that period, and his interpretation of Coleridge's personality differs from mine, so there seemed to be room for a further study of these six significant but comparatively unexamined weeks in the life of Coleridge and his friends.

London, 1972

Part I

Beckoning Hope

I · Friday 6th April

On a windy morning at the beginning of April 1804 two men got into a boat in Portsmouth harbour and were rowed out to a merchant brig at anchor at Spithead. The brig was expected to sail immediately, as part of a convoy bound for the Mediterranean. The squalls and hail-storms of the previous day had abated, and the wind was veering favourably, to north-north-east.

One of the men, Captain John Findlay, was short and fat-bellied, "a mild good sort of man, a Scotchman, prudent, well-meaning, unprofessing and plain" he seemed at first to his companion, who was to revise this straightforward character-sketch after a longer acquaintance. This companion, Samuel Taylor Coleridge, was a plump man of thirty-one, just under five feet ten in height, with undisciplined black hair and large wide-opened eyes of a clear slate-grey with no tinge of green or blue in them. He could not breathe through his nose, so his mouth always hung slightly open; its thick lips gave him a dolphin look. When he talked, his animated expression and his fine forehead and eyes made him attractive, but in repose his face looked chubby, boneless, dull. He considered himself an ugly man, fat-faced, awkward, almost idiotic-looking.

A fortnight earlier he had sat for his portrait to James Northcote. (Plate II). The sketch was done in two days, and with only one sitting, and that had to be broken off because Coleridge was suddenly taken ill; the painter finished the portrait next day without his sitter. But he caught something of Coleridge's speaking look, because during the sitting painter and sitter had had an argument about Milton—Northcote said he was ambitious and arrogant, which provoked Coleridge into a declaration that he was "next to Our Saviour in humility".

Opinions differed about the finished portrait. The painter and diarist Joseph Farington, who saw it the day it was finished and had dined in company with Coleridge the night before, thought it was very like; Coleridge himself reported that it was much admired; and the Wordsworths when they saw a print of it a year later thought the eyes and forehead and general outline a very good resemblance, though not the nose. But Coleridge's brother-in-law Southey strongly disapproved of it, and compared it unfavourably with a previous portrait of Coleridge by Hazlitt. "Hazlitt's does look as if you were on your trial, and certainly had stolen the horse; but then you did it cleverly, it had been a deep well-laid scheme, and it was no fault of yours that you had been detected. But this portrait by Northcote looks like a grinning idiot; and the worst is, that it is just like enough to pass for a good likeness, with those who only know your features imperfectly". It seemed to Southey that Northcote had caught the aspect of Coleridge that Southey liked and trusted least— the public performer, the man with a slightly rouged heart on his sleeve. Southey thought, and truly, that he knew another and better side of Coleridge, but he was too unsympathetic with that engaging public face.

When Coleridge got into the boat in Portsmouth harbour, he was warmly dressed in layers of clothes: two flannel waistcoats, with two other waistcoats on top of them under his coat, two pairs of flannel drawers under cloth pantaloons, thick yarn stockings. Marianne Dashwood, who despised the thirty-five-year-old Colonel Brandon for wearing a flannel waistcoat, the idea of which she "invariably connected with aches, cramps, rheumatisms, and every species of ailment that can afflict the old and the feeble", would have been even more shocked by the idea of a thirty-one-year-old poet wearing such a garment. But Coleridge was always afraid of the effects of sudden changes of temperature, which he believed to be the cause of the drastic bowel attacks to which he was subject; he had not yet allowed himself to recognize that these attacks were withdrawal symptoms of his opium addiction. He had another reason for being warmly clad as he set out. He did not expect much comfort or shelter in the ship in which he was to sail; the passenger accommodation was so small that he would have to spend most of the time on deck.

He had a good idea of what to expect, because a month earlier he had been on board the *Speedwell*, the merchant brig on which he had booked a passage to Malta, when she was in the London docks to load her cargo before she left for Portsmouth to join the convoy. She was a two-masted vessel of 130 tons; Coleridge called her "neat and compact" when he first saw her, and she was to prove a fast sailer though far from steady. She had a cargo of eighty-four large cannon in her hold, consigned to Trieste, and she was to call at Malta and Venice en route. She had accommodation for four passengers, but it was very cramped. It consisted of a single small cabin, "literally a box" Coleridge thought it, with curtained bunks, and the cabin had to serve as a dining-room for the captain and the passengers, as well as for sleeping in. Coleridge had to provide his own mattress, pillow, blankets and sheets for the voyage, and though food, tea and beer were included in the fare, he had to supply any other drinks. He and contributing friends of his laid in these on a very liberal scale: brandy, rum, wines and lemonade in special lockable travelling cases. Nevertheless he had to pay thirty-five guineas for his passage to Malta, a high but not unheard-of price by 1804 standards; but it was nearly a third of Coleridge's total secure annual income, and even today you can get to Malta for only £6 more.

After all, the convoy did not sail that Friday. On the previous evening the leading escort ship of the convoy, H.M.S. *Leviathan*, had signalled for all officers to come on board, and stand by for a signal gun to announce the moment of setting sail, and that morning the gale-force wind had dropped to moderate, and seemed to be setting in a favourable quarter. But during the day it veered to the west again, and the convoy's hopes of setting off down the Channel were quenched once more.

Coleridge suffered much anxiety and suspense from the alternation of postponements and urgent false alarms about the convoy's departure which he experienced after deciding to go on this voyage. The decision itself had taken three years to reach. As long ago as April 1801, after a winter of illness, he had planned to go to St Miguel in the Azores in search of health, and perhaps to stay there for some years. He was, he believed, faced with a momentous choice:

"Is it better to die or to quit my native Country, and live among Strangers?—Another winter in England would *do for me*". Unless he went abroad he had, he was convinced, no prospect of recovery. During the next few months he consoled himself with the thought of what the baths and the delicious climate of St Miguel would do for his "irregular gout", but by the end of July 1801 the plan had fallen through; money for his fare was lacking and the climate of the Azores was now reported to be unhealthily damp.

Three more winters in England did not in fact "do for him"; his health even improved a little between 1801 and 1804, though he was never well for long. Throughout these years he made ever-changing plans for tranquil sojourns abroad which were to "send me back to dear old England, a sample of the first Resurrection". He would go to Turkey or Egypt with Southey; he would settle for a time in a West Indian island, Nevis, St Lucia or Jamaica; he would accompany his ailing friend Tom Wedgwood to France or Spain; he would set off alone for Tenerife or Madeira.

Often his projects took the form of imagining an arcadian life on some sunlit shore with a colony of friends; this was a trailing cloud from the original dream of Pantisocracy, the community that was to have lived in wholesome joy on the green banks of the Susquehanna. The place and the cast of his new visions varied: he and his family would join Southey and his in Portugal; William and Dorothy Wordsworth would settle with the Coleridges in the Azores; Wordsworth, Southey, Humphry Davy, and perhaps Tom Wedgwood and James Tobin would make a little colony in Italy or the South of France; or perhaps he and Tom Wedgwood could take a house in Sicily, with the Wordsworths in another one next door, "in a genial climate a certain comfort of society among simple and enlightened men and women, your country folks". Would such an experiment have been as disastrous as the one planned by Byron, the Shelleys and the Leigh Hunts at Pisa? It was never tried: Coleridge's friends, though devotedly willing to uproot themselves and accompany him into exile, were in the end not called on for this.

The Wordsworths were as convinced as he was himself that his health would never be restored till he had lived for a time in a warm climate, but less partial friends suspected that the quest for health was not the whole story. "If your disease be really *bodily*, and not the consequence of an irritated mind, and if that bodily disease will be lessened or healed by a warmer climate, to a warmer climate you must go; but I never yet heard that complaints like yours were particularly alleviated by a warmer climate" wrote Thomas Poole bracingly. The disease was not all bodily. Coleridge was being seared by other corrosions: terrifying intermissions of poetic impulse, the raw decay of his marriage, unfulfilled love for another woman, unacknowledged servitude to opium. A new start, another chance to become the man he intended to be, was what he imperatively needed, and it seemed attainable if he could have a breathing-space of health and sunshine and freedom from responsibilities, "to which if I can add Tranquillity, the equivalent, and Italian climate, of the world within, I do not despair to be a healthy man".

He had to escape, but the choice of where to go was not easy. Money was short, reports about climatic conditions conflicted, and a European war was smouldering. The Treaty of Amiens gave hopes that France would be opened to British travellers, but by May 1803 England and France were at war again. Mediterranean possibilities were now reduced to Italy or Sicily; even Spain, though theoretically neutral, might not be safe. In August 1803 Coleridge began for the first time to consider a new corner of the Mediterranean, Malta, where an acquaintance of his, John Stoddart, had just been given a Government appointment and had invited Coleridge to visit him. Malta would be only a halting-place en route for Sicily, which he saw as his real destination. He hoped, by pulling strings, to get both a free passage to the Mediterranean and a free stay in Sicily. If he could get information well in advance as to which Royal Navy ship would be chosen to escort the next Mediterranean convoy—information which he hoped to have from a friend's friend in the Admiralty —he could get an introduction, through other influential friends, to the captain of the ship and be invited to travel to Malta as his guest. This casual hospitality in a warship in the middle of a naval campaign does not seem to have struck anyone as an unusual expectation. Coleridge's only fear was, not that he might find himself attending a sea battle, or that the request would be turned down as inappropriate in war-time, but that too many others would already have got in first with the same petition. He also expected, though he had no personal acquaintance either with Nelson or with Emma Hamilton, to get a letter of introduction from Nelson to the Benedictine monastery at Catania which would secure him free lodging there when he reached Sicily; and another from Lady Hamilton to the manager of Nelson's estates at Brontë.

By mid-March he had abandoned the hope of a free voyage in a warship, and had booked a passage in the *Speedwell*. Southey considered this a good thing. "You will be on the whole better off than in a King's ship. Now you are your own master; there you would have been a *guest*, and, of course, compelled to tolerate the worst of all possible society, except that of soldier-officers". This low rating of the company of naval officers is surprising from a man whose own brother was a naval lieutenant, and who was later to write the most celebrated of all the many biographies of Nelson.

Coleridge spent all the first three months of 1804 in an exhausting flurry of plans made and cancelled, of collecting advice and equipment and introductions. He had left Grasmere, where he had been staying with the Wordsworths, in mid-January; had spent two months staying with friends in London and Essex, dining out day after day with old and new acquaintances, being bowled over by sudden bouts of illness and picking himself up again, paying calls, writing letters, attending lectures and, through it all, talking in huge glistening loops of monologue.

On 24th March he heard that the *Speedwell* had left London on her way to Portsmouth, and that he must leave London by the 27th at the latest if he was to be sure of catching the *Speedwell* before she sailed from Portsmouth. Three of his friends, Charles Lamb, James Webbe Tobin, and Daniel Stuart, editor of the *Morning Post*, saw him off by the coach which left the Angel Inn in the Strand at seven o'clock on the evening of the 27th. Charles Lamb, who had a few days of Easter holiday owing to him from the East India House, intended to suggest going down to Portsmouth with Coleridge to see the last of him before he sailed. But before stammering Lamb could get in a word about this, Coleridge was buttonholed by Tobin, who was determined to give him some good advice and to reprove him about his bad habits. The farewell good wishes of Coleridge's closer friends, when he was about to leave England perhaps for years, were drowned in this flood of officious counsel, which was still booming in his ears as the coach drove out of London on the Portsmouth road. Then followed nine days of waiting in a noisy dirty inn at Portsmouth for the arrival of the *Speedwell*, and then for the wind to change so that the convoy could sail. By the time Coleridge finally got on board on 6th April, he was feeling stunned, almost deadened, by the hurly-burly of the last three months.

That evening on board, when the change of wind had again post-poned the sailing, Coleridge wrote a bread-and-butter letter to the friends with whom he had last been staying in London, the Beaumonts. In the cool and quiet of the ship at anchor, he thought over his recent experiences, and analysed how they had affected his state of mind, and he felt that a change was spreading through him, a change which was both a new departure and a home-coming, an escape by which he would find himself again, a star's fall into disconnection and the death-tranquillity of petrifaction, a star's return to its appointed welcome. In his letter to the Beaumonts he spoke of the fretting delay in sailing—perhaps it would be tomorrow, perhaps not for another fortnight—and of the turmoil of the last few months, the sudden transitions from country quiet to London drinkings and discussions and noise, the filth and raucous swearing surrounding him in Portsmouth, the violent bouts of illness which had discoloured his mind. "My spirits are low: and I suffer too often sinkings and misgivings, alienations from the Spirit of Hope, strange withdrawings out of the Life that manifests itself by existence—morbid yearnings condemn'd by me, almost despis'd, and yet perhaps at times almost cherish'd, to concenter my Being into Stoniness, or to be diffused as among the winds, and lose all individual existence". When he had written this, he paused, and began to take in his surroundings, to look out through the porthole and listen to the sea, and be conscious of a returning equipoise; and when he resumed his letter, it was to tell his friends—"Positively, this Night, that Star so very bright over the mast of a noble Vessel—and the sound of the water breaking against the Ship Side—it seems quite a *Home* to me".

II· *Saturday 7th April to Monday 9th April*

Next morning the crew of the *Speedwell* told Coleridge that they smelt a west wind, the contrary wind which had cancelled the sailing yesterday. So he went ashore again with Captain Findlay, enjoying the fine view of the sea and ships as he was rowed in. The sea was quite calm, as the wind had dropped still further, to a light breeze veering from west to south, and driving patches of sunlight and shade across the ships anchored at Spithead. As Coleridge was rowed ashore, he saw on one side the Isle of Wight, between the masts of a group of ships, and on the other side, towards the mainland, a splendid line of nine men of war with many smaller ships in between. Some had all sails set, others were reefed; the sunlight glinted and faded on their sails and on the roofs and spires of Portsea in the background, a pattern of shapes and colours which caught and then satisfied the eye.

Jane Austen saw Spithead and the ships on just such a day in spring a few years later, and she received such a prismatic impression that she introduced it as a scenic description, more vivid than was usual with her, in *Mansfield Park*. "It was really March; but it was April in its mild air, brisk soft wind, and bright sun, occasionally clouded for a minute; and everything looked so beautiful under the influence of such a sky; the effects of the shadows pursuing each other on the ships at Spithead and the island beyond, with the ever-varying hues of the sea, now at high-water, dancing in its glee". Turner, too, saw and painted Portsmouth and the ships on such a day, in a surging pattern of sheen and overcast. (Plate III).

Coleridge's ear, as well as his eye, was amused as he rowed

through the Fleet at Spithead. From the assembled ships came lively sounds of gun signals and salutes, the roll of drums, the bells, the shouted orders as anchors were weighed. Spithead was alive with ships as the convoys gathered themselves together for departure.

The Mediterranean convoy's escort ship, the *Leviathan*, was a 74-gun ship of the line which was being sent out to join Nelson's squadron in the watch on Toulon. Its Captain, Henry Bayntun, was a man of thirty-eight, son of a former British consul-general in Algiers. He had just returned from ten years' service in the West Indies, where he had been active and courageous in capturing several heavily armed French ships. As soon as he got back from the West Indies, he was posted to the *Leviathan*, with orders to take a big convoy of merchant ships out to the Mediterranean, and then to join the Fleet off Toulon. Nelson considered Bayntun an able and excellent officer, but he was rather too forthright and trenchant for the good of his career; on one occasion Nelson had to convey to him the displeasure of the Lords of the Admiralty at his style of writing. But as he later played a notable part at the Battle of Trafalgar, silencing several enemy ships and forcing the *St Augustin* to surrender, he ended up as a knighted admiral.

Fifteen merchant ships assembled at Spithead for this convoy; more were to join them later from other Channel ports. Some, like the *Harmony* and the *Ibbetson*, were colliers going out with coal for the warships in the Mediterranean; some, like the *Speedwell*, were taking cargo to Adriatic ports, or to Lisbon or Oporto. All that Saturday the convoy was poised for departure; the *Leviathan* moved further out in the direction of St Helens, and anchored in thirteen fathoms; and when Coleridge came on board the *Speedwell* again, the wind had shifted to the favourable quarter, and he felt confident that they would sail tomorrow if the wind held steady.

But on Sunday morning the wind was again variable. Coleridge stayed on board, and sat down to dinner with his fellow-passengers for the first time. There were two of them, Mr Hastings and Mrs Ireland. Hastings was a half-pay lieutenant who had become a merchant in a small way. His face, with its patches of yellow and purple, showed at first sight that he was a hard drinker. Mrs Ireland, who had been a housekeeper in a general's family, was even less prepossessing to look at. Coleridge wrote an astonished description after his first sight of her: "an unconscientiously fat Woman, who would have wanted Elbow Room on Salisbury Plain, a body that might have been in a less spendthrift mood of Nature sliced into a company, and a reasonable slice allotted to her as Corporal! I think, I never saw so large a woman, such a monopolist, patentee, abstract of superfluous Flesh!" With this repellent couple Coleridge was to share a single small cabin, for eating and for sleeping. He was to get amusement out of them, though, as well as irritation, and even to find them capable of some kindness and good sense.

That evening the wind at last settled in the east, and the *Speedwell* moved from Spithead to the station off St Helens in the Isle of Wight which was the assembly point for the convoy's start down the Channel. Everyone on board the *Speedwell* was now impatient about the delay in sailing; Coleridge was told that the wind would have enabled them to sail that morning if only the Commodore would have given the signal to the convoy.

It was not till half past seven on the morning of Monday 9th April that Captain Bayntun finally signalled to the convoy and the *Leviathan* weighed anchor. The wind, a fresh breeze, was then south-south-east, shifting to due east, and there was a haze. When the *Speedwell* weighed anchor to move off with the convoy, the crew grumbled so audibly that Coleridge described it as a "sort of mutiny". The ship was very short-handed, with less than half her complement of crew. Besides the Master, Captain Findlay, and the Mate, Mr Edridge, there were only four seamen, one of them a Swede, and two boys, one of whom was a negro; his white teeth, bright black eyes and cheerful black face attracted Coleridge and gave him an idea for a poem. When the *Speedwell* left London there had been three more seamen, but two of them had been seized by the press-gang in the Downs as the *Speedwell* was on her way to Portsmouth, and a third had run away at Portsmouth—"a rascal of a one-armed cook, better gone than stay'd", so Coleridge heard the crew say among their mutinous complaints as the anchor was hauled up.

Coleridge, who could get into conversation with absolutely anyone, was soon on friendly terms with all the *Speedwell*'s crew, and noted down many of their turns of phrase, their sea lingo, their weather-lore and superstitions. He was ignorant but curious about the technique of sailing a ship. The *Speedwell* was easy to sail, fast and nimble, but her motion was anything but easy for the passengers. The heavy cargo of cannon in the hold made her pitch and roll incessantly, with hiccuping jerks which gave continuous discomfort even to good sailors like Coleridge. He discovered a simile for this uneasy motion—it was as though a nurse, kept at home on a holiday to look after a fretful baby, rocked its cradle in vain to stop it screaming, and then went on rocking it violently, out of spite—and he liked his image so well that he used it in his letters about the voyage as well as recording it in his journal.

Coleridge was lucky in not suffering from seasickness, in spite of his general bad health. He had already discovered on his voyage from Yarmouth to Hamburg in 1798, his only previous sea voyage, that, while the Wordsworths and most of the other passengers were being disastrously seasick in a heavy storm, he was "neither sick nor giddy, but gay as a lark. The sea rolled rather high; but the motion was pleasant to me". On the *Speedwell* he never felt nausea from the movement of the ship, though occasionally one of her more violent pitches "jerked a dish of Tea out of my stomach by an action as merely mechanical, as it has more often jerked the Tea out of the cup", but he never had feelings of discomfort before or after. On this first morning at sea he felt sickish and feverish for a few hours, but was quite recovered by dinner-time, and ate a larger dinner than usual. Captain Findlay persuaded him to lie down on his bunk in the afternoon, which proved a mistake as it merely prevented him from sleeping well that night.

The convoy passed St Catherine's Point, the southernmost tip of the Isle of Wight, at noon, and with the fair breeze then blowing, it could have run down the Channel at nine or ten knots and made a good long start to the voyage. But more ships were due to join the convoy, so the Commodore anchored south-east of the Needles for the night. It proved a very uncomfortable night for Coleridge; the *Speedwell* pitched and rolled at anchor "like a Top Bough on a

Larch Tree in a high wind" and he got no real sleep, only feverish dozes, throughout the first night of his voyage.

At half past three in the morning of 10th April a small warship, the bomb *Thunder*, joined the convoy, and as they sailed down the Channel all that Tuesday more and more ships came out to meet the convoy from the South Coast ports, so that by sunset it consisted of thirty-six sail, with the *Leviathan* and two small bomb ships, *Thunder* and *Acheron*, as naval escort. St Alban's Head was sighted, and then the lights of Portland. The sky was cloudy, the sea fairly rough and the wind steady in the east.

The movement of convoys of merchant ships from Portsmouth to the Mediterranean was vital to Britain's prosperity in those war years, and was closely interlocked with the movements and needs of the British Fleet in the Mediterranean. A few months earlier the Admiralty had told Nelson, who was now commanding the Mediterranean Fleet, that there was little immediate prospect of relieving the line-of-battle ships then in the Mediterranean which needed to be sent home for a refit, but that, when possible, other line-of-battle ships would be sent out escorting convoys, so that Nelson could then gradually send home the ships needing to be overhauled. The despatch of the *Leviathan* with the convoy of 9th April was in accordance with the Admiralty's promise.

Escorting convoys was an arduous business. Commodores were instructed to proceed "as expeditiously as possible" but at the same time to "pay the most strict attention to the safety and protection of the Trade under your charge, that none of them may separate from you, or fall into the hands of the Enemy". Nelson considered the protection of British sea-borne trade as one of the Navy's most essential tasks; "for in no manner must the Trade of Great Britain be neglected" he added, in his own backward-leaning left-handed writing, to a letter giving convoy instructions which he had dictated to his secretary.

It was a precarious moment in the long war with France. All through the winter of 1803-4 Napoleon's *armée d'Angleterre* of a hundred thousand men had been encamped at Boulogne, with a flotilla of transports ready to carry them across the Channel. "All hearts anxious concerning the Invasion" Coleridge noted in October 1803, and Pitt had warned his auditors in a speech at Margate to expect the French every dark night. Men like Tom Wedgwood whose mother and sisters were living near the South Coast insisted on their moving to the north or west to escape the expected French invasion. Every man of military age was joining the volunteers; even Tom Wedgwood, sick man as he was, thought of doing so, but had to abandon the idea. Instead, he provided the money to raise and clothe a company of eighty men from among the Lake District farmers. Wordsworth attended a field day of theirs in May 1804, and dined with them in the open air on beef and plum pudding, and declared it to be the most interesting day he had ever witnessed. Enthusiasm and an exhilarating sense of crisis were the order of the day. Another friend of Coleridge's, Thomas Poole, who came up to London in December to head a Government enquiry, felt that he was at the nerve centre at a critical moment in world history; "we shall thus be all together, and all in the centre of action, during this interesting and bustling winter—a winter when a daring attempt will be made for the Empire of the world. We shall be able to lend our heads and our arms, I hope, to counteract this atrocious assault on the dignity of man" he told Coleridge.

By April 1804, when Coleridge left for Malta, the expectation of an immediate invasion had slightly faded, but the fear of it forced the Admiralty to keep at home some of the ships which Nelson so badly needed in the Mediterranean. The British Fleet there was fully extended by keeping watch on Toulon and the Spanish ports and by protecting convoys from privateers in the Straits of Gibraltar and all through to the Eastern Mediterranean, and had to envisage an extra threat, the possibility that neutral Spain, which was building up her fleet at Cadiz, might bring it into the war as France's ally, and join up with the French Fleet at Toulon. So far, Spain and Portugal were officially neutral, but their ports were closed to British warships. Most of Italy was also barred to the British. The French had subjugated Piedmont, Genoa and Leghorn—though this brought certain advantages too, as it meant that the British Fleet need not accord the rights of neutrality to ships from Genoa and Leghorn, and could use the Sardinian harbour of Maddalena, the King of Sardinia being against the French because of their seizure of Piedmont. Most of the Kingdom of Naples was occupied by French troops, and the Neapolitan Royal Family were again poised for possible flight from Naples to Palermo. The North African states, profiting by the quarrels of the European powers, gave shelter to privateers who preyed on merchant shipping, and went in for some near-piracy themselves; among all his other pre-occupations, Nelson had to spend part of the spring of 1804 negotiating with the Dey of Algiers, who had seized Maltese ships and crews, and had sent the British Consul packing on a trumped-up pretext.

Through this sequence of hazards, convoys like the one in which Coleridge sailed had to penetrate, on their way to deliver cargoes to the ports of the Adriatic and the Levant. The two narrow passages, at Gibraltar and between Sicily and Tunis, were the worst danger points for merchant shipping. The most effective warships for convoy protection were the fast-sailing frigates, but Nelson was dangerously short of frigates. Even including the three stationed outside the Straits of Gibraltar to keep watch over Cadiz, there were only eight of the smaller faster vessels, from 64-gun ships downwards to sloops, in the Mediterranean Fleet at this time. Nelson could have done with another ten frigates or sloops, but though he reported again and again to the Admiralty how "distressed for frigates" he was, he had to recognize that the Admiralty were unable or unwilling to increase his force. "I am pulled to pieces by the demands of merchants for convoys" he declared, and he had to work out the most elaborate time-tables for his few frigates to collect driblets of merchant ships here and there at each end of the Mediterranean and assemble them in large convoys, which could then travel from Gibraltar to the Levant, or vice versa, under the escort of a ship of the line and a sloop or two, which could protect them from privateers or from any French warship which might have slipped out from Toulon.

Though the protection of merchant convoys was an important preoccupation, Nelson's main job was the watch on Toulon. In the harbour of Toulon Admiral Villeneuve and his fleet of twenty-two ships, including ten ships of the line, were bottled up. It was Nelson's job to keep them constantly under surveillance, to tempt them out to battle if possible, and in any case to prevent their slipping out either westward, to escape into the Atlantic and join in an invasion of Britain, or eastward again towards Egypt and the gateway to the East. It was not a blockade, as Nelson often pointed out to those who congratulated him on having kept the French corked up in harbour. He wanted to get them out, not to keep them in; it was a cat-and-mouse operation. His tactics were to keep his main fleet out of sight of Toulon, thirty miles or so west, with a frigate closer inshore to watch the harbour mouth and report back to the Fleet if any ships emerged. He kept the French guessing about the movements of the British Fleet; it might be waiting just below the horizon, it might have gone to rendezvous with detached vessels, or to intercept Spanish reinforcements, to shelter under the lee of the Hyères Islands or to take on wood and water in Sardinia.

All through the winter and spring of 1803–4 Nelson moved his ships to and fro across his hunting-ground—from the Gulf of Lions to the Spanish Coast, south to the Balearics, east to Sardinia, north again into the Gulf. Most of his ships were battered and crazy after several years of Mediterranean service, and short of their full complement of men, and the wild winter gales of the Gulf were punishing. Topmasts or spars lost in storms could not be replaced by the depleted stores at Gibraltar and Malta, but under Nelson's instruction the ships off Toulon were so well handled that no one lost a topmast all winter, even in the worst gales. His own 2100-ton flagship, the *Victory*, with her 104 guns, crew of 850, and mainmast towering 175 feet from the deck, was comparatively new and in good condition, but four of the other ships of the line, *Kent*, *Superb*, *Triumph* and *Renown*, badly needed a refit, and so did some of the frigates.

But if decks and hulls in the Mediterranean Fleet were battered, morale was not. The day before Coleridge's convoy sailed from Portsmouth, Nelson was writing a letter about a rumour that the French Fleet was at sea. "I have only to wish to get alongside of them with the present Fleet under my command; so highly officered and manned, the event ought not to be doubted". He was fiercely proud of the courage and efficiency of his officers and men, and gave unceasing thought to the problems of protecting them from sickness, boredom and loss of heart during the gruelling months of sea patrols. He was too short of ships to spare any for rests in harbour, but he kept shifting their stations to give the ships' companies a taste of variety, and he took the greatest pains to ensure that their diet was healthy and balanced: plenty of beef; mutton for the sick; sweet oranges and onions, lemon juice and sugar to keep off the scurvy; and a special order of macaroni from Naples because he considered it a "light, wholesome, and nourishing food". He was fond of it himself, and often had a small plate of it for his abstemious dinner, but it is doubtful if he made many converts among the seamen. Beef was what they wanted, and attempts to interest them in any other diet—rice, for instance—were not successful. Nelson was constantly dictating letters about supplies of hammocks, coal, seamen's clothes; he even remembered to order Peruvian bark, or quinine, to be given twice a day to the men who went ashore on the malarial Sardinian coast for wood and water.

He took much less care of his own health. Besides the seasickness which always afflicted him in any storm, he was extremely thin, he had rheumatic pains from his amputated arm whenever the weather changed, and the sight of his remaining eye seemed to be going. But he stayed on deck, walking up and down, for six or seven hours a day, and sometimes all night, wearing thin clothes which he often did not change when they were soaked through, because getting off his clothes was difficult for a one-armed man and he did not want to trouble his servants to do it for him. It was a life of tension wrapped in monotony, for he never went ashore even when the *Victory* was in harbour. In April 1804 he had not set foot on land for nine months.

Nelson had been through an emotional entanglement like Coleridge's. He too had left behind in England an unloved nagging wife and another woman whom he passionately loved. But unlike Coleridge, he had slashed his way out of the entanglement, without any qualms or scruples. His wife had been given an irrevocable *congé*; Emma Hamilton had become his mistress and had already borne him a daughter Horatia, and now he had just received news of the birth of their second child, another girl, who did not survive, and also of Horatia's recovery from smallpox. On 10th April, as the *Speedwell* with Coleridge on board was beginning her voyage down the Channel, Nelson was writing from the *Victory* to Lady Hamilton, rejoicing over Horatia's recovery and also over Lady Hamilton's safe emergence from what he cautiously referred to as "your severe indisposition". He was convinced that his letters to Emma were read en route, so unless he could send them by a safe hand, he did not openly mention the parentage of Horatia and her sister. The fiction was employed that Horatia was a friend's child whom Lady Hamilton was kindly looking after. Nelson went on "I am glad that you are going to take my dear Horatia, to educate her. She must turn out an angel, if she minds what you say to her". But his confidence in the angelic nature of Emma's ideas, and even his longing to see her and Horatia, had not prevented him from greeting with horror a blithe suggestion from Emma that she and Horatia might join him aboard the *Victory* for a time. "Imagine what a cruize off Toulon is; even in summer time we have a hard gale every week, and two days' heavy swell. It would kill you; and myself to see you. Much less possible to have Charlotte, Horatia etc on board ship! And I, that have given orders to carry no woman to sea in the Victory, to be the first to break them!"

The only presence of Emma in the *Victory* which he could welcome and cherish was the portrait of her which hung in his cabin, and which he called his Guardian Angel. Painted in 1800, it showed a different image from the pliant nymph with loose chestnut locks painted by Romney fifteen years earlier. Emma's hair had darkened almost to black, and was worn in the short crisp curls of high fashion in the early 1800's. Her plump but still compact figure was almost primly dressed in a high-waisted gown with a white stock swathed round her neck nearly to her chin. She was still a very pretty woman, but calculation and pretence had already set marks on her face and posture. Only the eye of besotted love could have seen an angel in the portrait, though something of the nymph still enticed the spectator from the just-parted lips.

With this insistent presence in his cabin, Nelson always had Emma and Horatia in his thoughts. A few days after his letter to Emma about her recovery from childbirth, he sent a present to his child, with a covering note.

"My dear Horatia

I send you twelve books of Spanish dresses, which you will let your Guardian Angel, Lady Hamilton, keep for you, when you are tired of looking at them. I am very glad to hear that you are perfectly recovered; and, that you are a very good child. I beg, my dear Horatia, that you will always continue so; which will be a great comfort to
your most affectionate
Nelson and Brontë".

The daughter to whom this pathetic non-communication was addressed was a stout apple-cheeked child of three.

III · *Tuesday 10th April*

Late on Tuesday morning Coleridge came up on to the *Speedwell*'s deck to find that the weather was cool but clear and the sea rough. The convoy lay all around; he counted thirty-five ships ahead and astern, with gulls swooping and fishing between them. A blue coast-line was still visible to the right; Coleridge thought it was Start Point in Devonshire, but in fact the convoy was still only off Dorset, and it was probably St Alban's Head.

Coleridge felt so much better on deck in the fresh air that he decided that lying in his bunk only made him feel worse than he actually was, and that the thing to do was to have a plan of occupation for the voyage—"no Health or Happiness without Work". He decided to spend the morning on drawing up a daily programme, and he entered this in his journal. He would start the day, as soon as it was light and he was awake, by getting up, washing, and drinking hot ginger tea. Then till breakfast-time he would study Italian (with his Sicilian project in mind, he had brought with him a pocket Italian dictionary and grammar given to him by the Beaumonts, and the study of these was the only part of his daily programme that he really carried out during the voyage). After breakfast he would write or transcribe his journal, and then read Leibnitz's *Theodicée* and take notes on it for the book which he was at present engaged in writing. Then he would work till dinner-time on various essays and articles which he had in mind. Between dinner and tea he would read Italian, and after tea until bedtime he would try to compose some poetry. At the end of his note setting down this strenuous daily programme, he wrote "God grant me fortitude and a perseverant Spirit of Industry!"

He had brought a good supply of reading matter with him for the voyage: a book on mineralogy, works by Pascal and Marcus Aurelius, Leibnitz's *Essais de Theodicée sur la Bonté de Dieu, la liberté de l'homme et l'origine du mal*, and a 1686 folio edition of the works of Sir Thomas Browne, which had been much in Coleridge's mind recently—a month earlier he had sent a long critical analysis of them to his beloved, Sara Hutchinson. He may also have had with him on the voyage a copy of Dante's *Divina Commedia*.

The most important of these books for his present purposes was Leibnitz's work, because ideas from it were to be included in the book on which Coleridge himself was now working. The first idea of this book had come to him over a year earlier, in a rather trivial form—a notion for a "pretty book, entitled 'Le Petit Soulagement, or Little Comforts, by a Valetudinarian'—comprising cookery, sleeping, travelling, conversation, self-discipline, poetry, morals, metaphysics—all the alleviations, that reason and well-regulated self-indulgence can give to a good sick man". This attractive project for a bedside book had evolved by the end of 1803 into a much more serious and philosophical design: a work which was to be resonantly entitled *Consolations and Comforts from the exercise and right application of the Reason, the Imagination, and the Moral Feelings, addressed especially to those in Sickness, Adversity, or Distress of*

C

Mind, from speculative Gloom. The last two words of the title dis-
satisfied him, indeed he considered them barbarous, but though he
had puzzled over this for hours he could not hit upon any other
phrase which would concisely express his exact meaning.

In a letter to Sir George Beaumont he gave a full account of the
themes which were to make up his work. The *Consolations* were to be
for the miserable: practical advice for the sick and the unfortunate,
philosophical counsel for the distressed in mind, for whom he hoped
to provide "a new Theodicée, and what will perhaps appear to many
a new Basis of Morals". The *Comforts* were to be for the happy and
prosperous, and would suggest to them new sources of enjoyment—
better, more various and more numerous than the common ones.

The book was well under way by November 1803, when Southey
described it with the mixture of envy, admiration and derision which
he reserved for his brother-in-law's activities. "He is arranging
materials for what, if it be made, will be a most valuable work, under
the title of 'Consolations and Comforts', which will be the very
essential oil of metaphysics, fragrant as otto of roses, and useful as
wheat, rice, port wine, or any other necessary of human life". Coleridge continued working on the book when he was staying with the
Wordsworths at Grasmere at the beginning of January 1804, before
he left for London and Malta, and he told Southey that he had filled
a third of a large notebook with hints, thoughts, facts and illustrations
for the book.

The notebook which he was using at that time contains only a few
entries which Coleridge specifically identifies as being for *Consolations and Comforts,* but there are many others which seem to have a
bearing on its subject, and which Coleridge may have earmarked as
hints and illustrations for the book. It is hard to make a summary of
these without giving a platitudinous effect, above which Coleridge
himself would have soared if he had written the complete book. It
can be discerned that Coleridge meant to suggest to the suffering and
the unhappy that they could win distraction from their pains by
generalizing from their individual cases, by unveiling the vividness
of their own ideas and memories so that these blotted out dark
corners of the mind, above all by choosing, cherishing and strength-

ening the pleasurable sensations which they derived from the observation of natural beauty. Many intricate analyses of Westmorland landscapes in the winter of 1803–4, included in this notebook, may have been intended to go into *Consolations and Comforts* to illustrate this point; as when in November in Borrowdale, looking along Bassenthwaite to the range of wintry hills, the lower ones black, the higher peaks dazzling white in deep snow and wreathed in clouds, he noted "the *choice* of sensations, I in much pain leaning on my Staff, and viewing the clouds and hearing the Church Bell from Crosthwaite Church".

He meant, too, to encourage the wretched to distract their minds, as he himself often did, by the very act of observing their own mental operations, and to explore their own consciousness and identity. Of the man who achieved this it might be said, Coleridge suggested, that "he looked at his own Soul with a Telescope; what seemed all irregular, he saw and shewed to be beautiful Constellations and he added to the Consciousness hidden worlds within worlds". Such men would come to realize how their physical and mental faculties shaded into each other, how the darkest of moral and intellectual eclipses might be the birth-pangs of new virtues, how the soul might grow during the sleep of death. Thence the reader would be led on to more general speculations about the origin of moral evil, and to that "new basis of morals" which Coleridge had half worked out from his mental arguments with Kant about the virtuous will and the desire of happiness. These counsels would have been lightened and varied by Coleridge's brilliant idiosyncrasy of illustration; it seems probable, for instance, that those (among whom Coleridge included himself) who were made unhappy by their own ugliness would have been consoled by the reminder that judgements on personal beauty depend on convention; Tartar chieftainesses cut off the tops of their noses to make their faces look more appealingly flat.

In mid-January Coleridge told Thomas Poole that he had been purposively busy with this book for the last three months, "and I want only one fortnight's steady Reading to have got *all* my materials before me—and then I neither stir to the Right or to the Left, so

35

help me God! till the Work is finished". Poole was sufficiently impressed to make suggestions about a publisher for the book, and Coleridge was quite ready to start discussions about this. At the beginning of February he told Sir George Beaumont that he had now finished collecting the materials for the book and it would be ready for the printers within three months. He added "Of this work every page has and will come from my Heart's Heart—and I may venture, dear and honored Friends! to say to you, without dreading from you the Imputation of Vanity, that what I have written is to my own mind a pure Strain of Music".

Two months later, on board the *Speedwell* in mid-Channel, he was still including the taking of notes for his *Consolations and Comforts* as a job to be fitted into his plan of work for the voyage. He had described his book as "a new Theodicée", and the notes he meant to take now were from the original *Theodicée*, Leibnitz's celebrated study of omnipotence, free will and the origin of evil. Parts of the *Theodicée* make it easy to see why Coleridge thought of it as a source of ideas which would enable the afflicted to win consolation by rightly using their reason, imagination and moral feelings. Leibnitz's elegant lucidity, his well-bred equanimity, at times make it understandable that he should have been on Coleridge's short-list of men whom one looked forward to meeting in Heaven; a very odd list it was, including—besides the foreseeable names of Shakespeare and Milton—Luther, the mathematician Bernouilli and the naturalist Charles Bonnet. On another occasion Coleridge classed Leibnitz with Plato and Zeno among the "sublimest teachers of moral wisdom". But he also at one point described Leibnitz's main theory as "glaringly repugnant to Common Sense", and there is little evidence to suggest which passages in the *Theodicée* Coleridge may have singled out for his own book during the voyage to Malta. Perhaps he may have marked for quotation the beautiful passage on love and reason in the Preface to the *Theodicée*, which declares that the most agreeable of pleasures is loving that which is worthy of love, and this true charity makes us concentrate on what is noblest in other men. Coleridge always aspired to fix his heart on the good elements in his fellow-men and in their works, even when his intelligence was surveying all elements. He despised the critic's trick of selective quotation from a writer's works in order to depreciate them, and greatly admired Leibnitz's large-minded way of always concentrating on the best and truest parts of other men's works, on the area of agreement and affirmation, not the area of difference and denial. There was certainly material there which could be included among techniques for consolation.

Consolations and Comforts was never finished, either on the Malta voyage or afterwards. It was not all lost; drafts and quotations intended for it later found their way into Coleridge's periodical *The Friend*, and into *Biographia Literaria*, at which in a sense he worked for at least seventeen years before it finally appeared. But it is hard not to mourn the loss of the original project for *Consolations and Comforts*, the unheard melody of that "pure strain of music". Perhaps Coleridge's techniques of consolation would work only with those whose bent of mind qualifies them for such techniques, and who are therefore likely to be practising them already. But one imagines that little volume—a medley of quotations, aphorisms, and descriptions, something about the length of *Biographia Literaria*, but brighter in image and colour, more of a young man's book—as something that one might indeed have kept at hand if one were ill, wretched or depressed, and have treasured as a favourite travelling book, like *Texts and Pretexts* or *The Unquiet Grave*.

Coleridge's daily programme for the voyage prescribed work on the *Consolations and Comforts* in the morning, but the composing of poetry after tea. Ideas for poems, suggested by the life of the ship, drifted into his head: a lullaby song for a child at sea, or a dirge for the negro ship-boy; a *jeu d'esprit*, an afterpiece, a "voyage in verse", a sequence of strange thoughts and sights from dreams; momentary insights from birds and waves, moonlight and patterns of rigging. Some of these attached themselves to poems already written or projected, for instance to *The Soother of Absence*, which had been originally conceived as a topographical poem linked with the Lake District, but had evolved into a sequence of poems on happy and unhappy love. One poetic task he had, on which he made no progress during the voyage, although the hope of completing it had been one of the impulsions to his journey. In March he had assured Lady Beaumont, who had just read all of *Christabel* that he had so far written, that "the thought that you and Sir George will at times talk of the poem by your fire side, or in your summer evening walks, and sometimes wish for its conclusion, will be one and a strong inducement to me, to finish it". Another friend was told that he hoped to finish both *Christabel* and *The Dark Ladie* before he reached Malta. When he drew up his programme, he intended that the quiet hours before bedtime during the voyage should be above all dedicated to the completion of *Christabel*, which had been at a standstill since 1800. But it did not work out like that.

What did Coleridge himself feel, by the time he left for Malta, about the haleness of his poetic powers? There is no shortage of evidence for his feelings about this between 1800 and 1804; there is indeed all too much, half of it contradicting the other half. When he had finished the second part of *Christabel* in September 1800, he announced flatly that he was going to abandon the writing of poetry altogether, and to devote himself to propaganda for the poetry of Wordsworth and Southey, and two months later he confirmed this abandonment, "being convinced", as he bitterly added, "that I never had the essentials of poetic Genius, and that I mistook a strong desire for original power".

For a man who had abandoned poetry, he produced a surprising amount in the next three years, including the great *Dejection*, the haunting *Pains of Sleep*, and most of the poems to Sara Hutchinson. His biographers, and he himself in his letters, have devoted much space to the many works which he promised but failed to write, but what he actually did complete and publish was not a negligible output. His own conviction about his poetic calling was undulant. At the beginning of March 1801 he had cheerful and confident hopes of himself as a poet; three weeks later he was writing "The Poet is dead in me". His hopes were low in 1802—"all my poetic Genius, if ever I really possessed any *Genius*, and it was not rather a mere general *aptitude* of Talent, and quickness in Imitation, is gone" (this was only three months after writing *Dejection*); and lower still in June 1803—"it seemed a Dream, that I had ever *thought* on

Poetry—or had ever written it". But five months later he was drawing up a huge list of the poems he intended to write, and in the spring of 1804 his letters are full of confidence (perhaps slightly forced in tone) in his future literary achievements once his health had been re-established by his sojourn abroad.

There is no agreement among Coleridge's biographers and critics as to whether or not his poetic inspiration failed him for good in the early 1800's, and if so, why it did. It used to be taken for granted that all the real interest of Coleridge's life was crammed into the years before 1802. Then a reaction of scholars, impatient at the ignoring of his later prose, focused critical attention on Coleridge the philosopher-psychologist-critic. At present there seems to be a slight swing back towards the failure-of-inspiration theory, now attributed to sexual impotence, or frustrated love for Sara Hutchinson, or Wordsworth's lack of sympathy, or opium addiction, or disappointed hopes of mystical experience (or conversely, to the freezing effects of growing orthodoxy in religion).

We now at least know what Coleridge wrote and did not write in the last thirty years of his life. In 1804, when he left for Malta, he could not know what lay ahead, but he was optimistic. "I am eager to hope all good things of my health—and that gained, I have a cheering, and I trust, prideless Confidence, that I shall make an active and perseverant use of the faculties and acquirements, that have been entrusted to my keeping, and a fair Trial of their Heighth, Depth, and Width".

IV · *Tuesday 10th April to Wednesday 11th April*

"What a beautiful object a single wave is!" wrote Coleridge in his notebook after watching the Channel surges shouldering past the hull of the *Speedwell* and hastening on towards the ring of convoy

ships, with the white gulls skimming above the wave-crests like
upflung spray.

Patterns of moving foam had always fascinated Coleridge. On his
first sea voyage, to Hamburg in 1798, he leant over the ship's side at
night, absorbed in watching the foam clouds darting away from the
bows, with stars of phosphorescence curvetting in their tracks. A
year later he pored over an "eddy-rose" of white foam on the river
Greta near its fall into the Tees; watching it form itself again and
again in the swift downward rush of the stream, he said to himself
that it was "obstinate in resurrection . . . endless variety in Identity".
On his voyage to Malta he was never weary of watching the patterns
of the waves as they lifted into crests of foam and sank in wrinkled
slopes down to deep troughs, and swelled again in dimpling ripples
to flash sun-glints from their summits. How could anything be so
sharply defined and yet so perpetually changing, have such endless
variety in identity, utterly distinct and yet an undivided unity? "I
particularly watched the beautiful Surface of the Sea in this gentle
Breeze! every form so transitory, so for the instant, and yet for that
instant so substantial in all its sharp lines, steep surfaces, and hair-
deep indentures, just as if it were cut glass, glass cut into ten
thousand varieties, and then the network of the wavelets, and the
rude circle hole network of the Foam". He tried to snatch the exact
look of the sea surface, in phrases and images scribbled into his
notebook. Many of them were images of minerals—the waves had
the sheen of soapstone, bright reflections such as he had seen on
fireplaces of plumbago slate, the exquisite purple of tinted drinking
glasses, shimmers of brass and polished steel and tin alloys. He was
remembering Humphry Davy's lectures on chemistry at the Royal
Institution which he had attended two years earlier, and on which he
took copious notes, full of excitement at the glitter and colour of the
chemicals used in the experiments accompanying the lectures. Now
as he looked at the lustrous surface of the sea, he remembered the
zinc and lead, copper and tin and steel, that had been used in Davy's
experiments, and how they had glowed and sparkled.

All that Tuesday as the convoy ran down the Channel with a
fresh easterly breeze, under a cloudy sky, the waves spread their

patterns from ship to ship, and Coleridge's eyes followed their con-
volutions and iridescent hues. At daylight on Wednesday the convoy
was five leagues south-west of Bolt Head. At ten o'clock the
Leviathan set more sail, and by noon Dodman Point in Cornwall
was three or four leagues to the north-west. Just after two they came
to the wind on the larboard tack off Falmouth, where the *Etna* and
some more merchant ships were to join the convoy. By eight in the
evening they were emerging from the Channel, with the Lizard
light to their north-west, but two hours later the convoy was held
up by a mysterious incident, laconically recorded in *Leviathan*'s log.
"At ten hove to and sent a boat on board the Speculation brig,
found the Master dead and sent a man on board to assist them".

If Coleridge got word of this, it would have strengthened the
paramnesia which beset his whole voyage. He had been here before,
he had already lived through this, in a prophetic vision which he had
imagined and written down before he had ever left the shores of
England, the vision of the Ancient Mariner's voyage. When he
wrote the poem, Coleridge probably did not consciously identify
himself with the Mariner; any identification, and that at a very
deep level, was rather with the ship and its dependence on the wind.
But for a year or more before he left for Malta, Coleridge had begun
to see his Mariner as a projection of his own growing isolation and
unhappiness, and to hope like the Mariner for a liberating wind to
carry him away. Too much can be made of this; it has been suggested
that the Mariner's weight of guilt was shared by Coleridge on this
voyage, that his forbidden love for Sara Hutchinson, his jealousy of
Wordsworth, and his opium addiction haunted his conscience and
suffused with fear the sea sights and sounds which he observed on
the voyage, and afterwards used when he revised *The Ancient
Mariner*. But at least in the first part of this voyage, Coleridge was
still hopeful and often happy. He had set out to achieve a rebirth of
health and inspiration, but he had not acknowledged any radical
guilt calling for repentance. If he had shot an albatross, it had not
yet been hung round his neck.

When Coleridge had *déjà vu* feelings during the voyage as he
watched and listened to his surroundings, some of them were the

pleasure of an author when later observation confirms that he has imagined true. He saw the evening star dogging the crescent moon, the outlines of distant sails like gossamer against the horizon, the coiling gleams of light in the shadow of the ship; he heard the crew gossiping about their superstitions, and saw their unthinking cruelty to a bird that wheeled from ship to ship seeking rest; and felt that his visionary insights in *The Ancient Mariner* had been authentic. He was also assimilating new observations, for later use, and when he published a revised version of *The Ancient Mariner* thirteen years later, he altered some lines to tally more closely with sea realities, and added a stanza based on his glimpse of the gleam upcast by the steersman's lamp onto the *Speedwell*'s mainsail.

The finest of the additions made in 1815–16 to *The Ancient Mariner* originated on this night of 10th April when Coleridge was on the *Speedwell*'s deck watching the sky and remembering the stars he had seen four nights earlier at Spithead, and the feeling of home-coming that had been with him then. Now the heavens seemed to him to be full of joyful and illustrious movement. "The Ship at night moves like the crescent in a firmament of Clouds and Stars in them, the Clouds now all bright with a moonlike Light, now dim and watery-grey—now darting off—and often at such distance that they lose all apparent connection with the Ship, and seem each its own Lord, Spirits playing with each other. . . . I observed close under the Ship side, a constant clear blue Sky with coursing Stars". That cluster of images and emotions remained in his mind, growing more and more charged with his own sense of isolation and stag-nation, till the moment when he was revising *The Ancient Mariner* for re-publication, and then he added the most beautiful of all the glosses beside the stanza about the Mariner watching the moon rise:

"In his loneliness and fixedness he yearneth towards the journey-ing Moon, and the stars that still sojourn, yet still move onward; and everywhere the blue sky belongs to them, and is their appointed rest, and their native country and their own natural homes, which they enter unannounced, as lords that are certainly expected, and yet there is a silent joy at their arrival".

V · *Wednesday 11th April*

Coleridge spent part of Wednesday in unpacking his trunk. As he expected to be away for at least a winter, he had brought a good many possessions with him. There were his books and notebooks, his wine and spirits. He had brought quite a trousseau of clothes, including light-weight ones—white silk stockings, washable waist-coats, nankeen pantaloons—to wear in the Mediterranean heat, and green spectacles to protect his eyes from the strong sunlight. He had brought mustard and ginger powder, concentrated lemon and portable soup, and his own knife and fork, to supplement the fare provided on board ship. He had a stock of medicines: James's powder, turkey-rhubarb, quinine, smelling salts, court-plaister— and an ounce of crude opium and nine ounces of laudanum in a stout travelling-bottle. As he dug about in his trunk among all these possessions, he came on the little lockable escritoire which Lady Beaumont had given him before he sailed. He had described its elegance proudly in a letter to Southey, as evidence of the Beaumonts' flattering cares for him, but he had not really looked into it then, though a farewell letter from Lady Beaumont had re-minded him of its carefully-packed but incongruous contents—a packet of James's powder in the drawer, and manuscript copies of Wordsworth's poems in the middle part. Now, on board the *Speedwell*, Coleridge examined his present properly, and was delighted with it. "I had never connected any pleasure with neatness and convenience; now for the first time they seized my Heart at once by a hundred Tentacula of Love and affection and pleasurable Remembrances. How could it be otherwise? Every thing had been so manifestly placed there by the Hand of affectionate Solicitude!"

Coleridge had good reason for his warm feelings about the Beaumonts; they had been very kind to him. If one were allowed to choose among all the possible English houses in which to stay during the early years of the nineteenth century, perhaps one would choose to stay with the Beaumonts. Their hospitality was praised alike by Walter Scott, easiest of guests—who called Sir George Beaumont "by far the most sensible and pleasing man I ever knew"—and by Benjamin Robert Haydon, one of the most difficult guests imaginable, who was allowed by the Beaumonts to paint all day and talk about painting all through every meal while he stayed with them. The Beaumonts' various houses were extremely comfortable, always full of interesting guests, and hung with pictures some of which are now among the chief treasures of the National Gallery—paintings by Poussin, Claude Lorrain, Rembrandt, Canaletto, and Rubens's *Château de Steen.*

Sir George Beaumont, seventh baronet with a distinguished royal and poetic ancestry which impressed Coleridge in spite of his dislike of privilege, was a man of fifty-one when Coleridge stayed with him before leaving for Malta. He had been married for twenty-six years to Margaret Willes, an enthusiastic round-cheeked woman with a slight stammer and dark eyes often shining with tears of emotion over music or poetry. Sir George himself was high-nosed, long-faced, his eyebrows well shaped on a handsome forehead. He was celebrated for the unselfconscious urbanity of his manners, for his droll but good-natured anecdotes, for his considerate kindness, and for his artistic flair. He was himself a pleasing unadventurous landscape painter, but his greatness was as a connoisseur.

When Beaumont first met Coleridge in 1803 he disliked him very much, and made plans to avoid him in future. Coleridge himself knew this, and bore no resentment about it afterwards; he valued a slowly deepening affection more than a sudden hot liking. As Beaumont heard more of Coleridge's conversation, he began to admire and value him. From August 1803 onwards the two men corresponded, and when Coleridge came south at the beginning of 1804, the Beaumonts asked him to stay. At this time their main house, at Coleorton in Leicestershire, was uninhabitable; the old house had been pulled down and a new one designed by George Dance was to be built, but its foundation stone was not laid till August of that year. The Beaumonts were therefore mainly living in their London house in Grosvenor Square. When they wanted country quiet, they stayed with Sir George's mother at the Clock House at Dunmow in Essex, a smallish Elizabethan manor house of red brick with mullion windows, Dutch gables, and a little pepper-pot clock tower above the front door. It stood on a gentle slope, with a prospect of fields and a church tower.

It was here that Coleridge stayed with them for ten days in February 1804, soothed by their kindness and hospitality. "Their solicitude of attention is enough to effeminate one. Indeed, indeed, they *are* kind and good people—and Old Lady Beaumont, now 86, is a sort of miracle for beauty, and clear understanding, and chearfulness". It was a happy stay, during which the friendship matured into real confidence; Lady Beaumont talked to Coleridge about her early life and feelings, her techniques of prayer, and he told her about his children. They turned over Sir George's portfolios of drawings and sketches, and Coleridge made notes on them for a projected publication of poems and drawings together. And they joined their admirations for Wordsworth, talking of his domestic happiness and his poetic genius till Lady Beaumont's ready tears glistened on her cheeks.

When Coleridge returned to London in mid-February, the Beaumonts' kindnesses continued. Sir George gave him an introduction to Richard Payne Knight, who would be able to get him a letter from Lady Hamilton to Nelson's agent at Brontë. As soon as the Beaumonts got back to London from Dunmow in mid-March, they sought out Coleridge again, and as he had a bad attack of what he called cholera morbus that weekend, they got him to come and stay in Grosvenor Square, and looked after him assiduously till he left for Portsmouth a week later.

They gave a dinner-party during his stay, which one of the guests, the painter Joseph Farington, described at length in his diary that night. Farington was a conventionally minded dictatorial man, contemptuous of ideas and conversations which he had not properly understood. He was not impressed by Coleridge who, he considered, dominated the conversation too much, was too metaphysical, and had a broad Devonshire accent. Farington's rather flat summary of the topics discussed—techniques of painting and poetry, the classic orders in architecture, the dangers of novel-reading, ghost stories, ocular spectra—gives far less idea of the magic of Coleridge's talk than Keats's famous and not dissimilar summary of Coleridge's monologue to him in 1819. Farington does, however, record one sentence which sounds like Coleridge's own words—a description of Erasmus Darwin's inexpert plagiarism "like a pigeon picking up peas, and afterwards voiding them with excrementitious additions".

Coleridge's comment on Farington was terser but not less contemptuous than Farington's on Coleridge. Spelling Farington's name wrong, and referring to a folio on towns in Wales which he had published, Coleridge wrote in his journal that weekend "Mr Farringdon's *conscientious* views of North Wales".

The Beaumonts' attentions to Coleridge lasted right up to his departure. They equipped him with books and drinks and travelling gadgets and had them packed for him, they commissioned Northcote to do a portrait of him before he left, and sent a servant to see him and his luggage on to the Portsmouth mail. Coleridge, who had not moved much in a world where it was normal to be packed for and seen off at stations by a servant, was rather overwhelmed by it all, and wrote emotional notes of thanks to the Beaumonts. Sir George replied with well-bred warmth. "If good wishes innumerable can accelerate a passage yours will be the shortest that was ever made to Malta—Never again mention obligations to us—believe me, and from my soul I speak it, the advantages Lady Beaumont and myself have gained from you and Wordsworth more than a million times repay the trifling attentions we had it in our power to show you both". His opinion of Coleridge had now entirely altered from his first unfavourable impression, and he thought of this, in a Jane-Austen-like phrase, as "an instance why we should not give way to first prejudices". He still thought Coleridge not equal to Wordsworth in poetic power, though better-read and more learned, but he reckoned himself fortunate to have encountered such a genius, and was impressed by Coleridge's true and humble reverence for Wordsworth. As for Lady Beaumont, she could hardly express what she felt on parting from Coleridge, but she asked him to pray for her.

VI · *Wednesday 11th April*

When Coleridge had finished his unpacking, he dined abstemiously off soup and vegetables, and then went up on deck. The *Speedwell* was at the centre of the convoy, which was tacking off Falmouth. The wind had dropped a little, and the sky was cloudy; presently it began to rain, and Coleridge felt drowsy and stupefied. He ate nothing more that day, but his sleep that night was disturbed by a nightmare. The dream began pleasantly enough; he saw Sir Philip Sidney's wife talking to her maid about her husband. But he was not sure of her identity—perhaps she was Harriet Byron, heroine of Samuel Richardson's novel *Sir Charles Grandison*. The lovely creature, whoever she was, vanished, and now Coleridge was in a dark passage where three ghostly old women were attacking him, terrifying him so much that he woke screaming.

Coleridge attributed his afternoon of drowsiness and stupor and his night of bad dreams to the change in the weather, the onset of rain. This was his standard explanation of the violent bowel attacks, accompanied by vomiting, sweats, yawning and faintness, which laid him low every few weeks. "This is ever the way with me; Rainy windy Weather diseases my stomach". He had persuaded himself that laudanum was the only certain cure for these attacks, and shield against nightmares, and this was indeed true, though not in the way he thought; since his attacks were withdrawal symptoms from opium, only a further dose of opium could stop them.

He had diagnosed his complaint as possibly some form of scrofula, but more probably a kind of rheumatic gout, not true gout but "primarily a Disease of the Skin, and affecting the Digestive organs by the diseased Action of the Skin". He maintained that he was an absolute slave to the weather, that when it was bad he could only keep off illness by taking opiates, and that he had not detected any pernicious effects from taking them. This was disingenuous, for in another letter only two days later he had admitted that opium, though it had other good effects, did have one bad one—it disorganized his stomach unless he took a large dose; and shortly before leaving for Malta he confided to his notebook that "Opium always in the day-time increases the puffing Asthma, eye closing, and startlings".

Coleridge was suffering from two separate evils, one natural and one artificially induced, and was trying to explain two separate sets of symptoms by a single diagnosis. He had some form of gout which caused acutely painful swellings in his knees and ankles, and outbreaks of ulcers and boils. This began in 1800–1, and he started taking opium regularly as an anodyne for the fierce pain which he suffered from the gout at this time, though he already knew from experience that opium had other charms and solaces for him. His other most pronounced symptom in the following years—the alternation of extreme costiveness with violent diarrhoea—was due to indulgence in, and then temporary abstinence from, opium. His susceptibility to weather changes was only a convenient excuse, though he did not at this stage recognize the opium withdrawal symptoms—diarrhoea, asthmatic breathing, yawning, restlessness, cramps, insomnia—unmistakably for what they were.

Nor had he traced any connection between his opium-taking and his nightmares; on the contrary, he justified his nightly opium doses as a specific against the frightful dreams which he so much dreaded. In fact, both his nightmare of the old ghosts attacking him in the dark passage, and the stupefied drowsiness which preceded it on this Wednesday afternoon, were probably due to an extra or premature dose of laudanum which he had taken when his morning's unpacking brought to light his supplies of the drug.

Coleridge's nightmares were horrible. In them raged and cringed a self which he could not bear to acknowledge. The dream Coleridge was tortured by loathing desire for abominable creatures which inflicted agonies of mutilation and infection on him. Excruciated by injustice and the triumphs of enemies, he yearned for vengeance, but his boasting and struggles were futile, and ended in craven flight from his persecutors—or were they persecutors? Was it not

I Passengers embarking and landing in Portsmouth Harbour. *Drawing by Thomas Rowlandson, 1816*

II Samuel Taylor Coleridge. *James Northcote, 1804*

he himself who had done the secret crime, and was now being hunted for it? He was stifled by vile terror, and his only rest was in despair, the passive and endless despair that the damned in hell suffered.

We have to take Coleridge's word for it that he experienced these extremities of suffering in dreams, for the dreams themselves as he describes them have little of this apocalyptic horror, though they wrung shrieks of fear from a grown man. He himself was puzzled by the disproportion between the events of his dreams and the emotions which they aroused. "In a distempered dream", he wrote, "things and forms in themselves common and harmless inflict a terror of anguish". He made many notes about his dreams and nightmares; ghastly as they were—a recurring nightly torture which made him afraid to go to bed—they still aroused his unquenchable intellectual curiosity. Why should the mind suffer such contortions? How were they operated? A meditation on dreams was one of the projects floating in his mind in the winter before he left for Malta, and throughout the voyage he went on making notes on his dreams, and his psychological deductions from them.

How much of the reason and the will persisted in dreams? He had observed in himself the dream-about-a-dream pattern, in which his mind analysed in a dream the events of an earlier dream. He knew that during a nightmare he could will himself to scream, and so wake himself. In his shallow restless sleeps he was aware of his own will still acting, but his half-conscious mind sometimes transferred the act of intention to his inanimate surroundings; the surge of the ship which rolled him from one side of his bunk to the other seemed to be directed by his brain giving orders to his muscles. The reaction between external stimuli and the dreaming mind was a leading theme of his meditations on dream-work. A ticking watch at the bedside or the pressure of crumpled sheets had transformed themselves into dream incidents; so had indigestion. On one night during the voyage Coleridge had a thought just as he was falling asleep which he described as "a really important Hint". This was "the effect of the posture of the Body, *open mouth* for instance, on first Dreams—and perhaps on all. White Teeth in behind an open

D

mouth of a dim face. My Mind is not vigorous enough to pursue it—but I see, that it leads to a development of the effects of continued Indistinctness of *Impressions* on the Imagination according to laws of Likeness".

Here was the real reason for Coleridge's studies of dreams. There was nothing intrinsically interesting about a ticking watch or a bout of indigestion, and not much of interest in the dreams that they produced. But by watching these sub-conscious and semi-conscious movements of the imagination, something might be deduced about those other movements which produced poetry. During this voyage Coleridge drew an important analogy: poetry was a rationalized dream. As in dreams, feelings of which we are not fully conscious are made real to us in poetry by symbols. The beings and events of Coleridge's dreams told him things about himself of which he was unaware, but this was an involuntary process. The poet, using his reason, can consciously operate his imagination by the same technique.

The imagination at work with the "laws of likeness", with identity in difference, with the creation of symbolic equivalents, was the aspect of dream-work which interested Coleridge most of all during the voyage. Not all his dreams were nightmares; some of them were sweet and moving experiences of the presence of those whom he loved. But they seldom appeared in their actual physical likenesses. In his dreams he saw men and women whose appearance, character and speech were quite unlike anyone that he knew, but nevertheless he was sure of their identity—they were old school friends of his, they were William or Dorothy Wordsworth, they were his wife and children. This "*feeling* of a Person quite distinct at all times, and at certain times *perfectly separable* from, the Image of the Person" could attach itself not only to an alien appearance, but even to a series of events, a whole long story in a dream in which the person neither appeared nor was concerned, and yet the whole dream seemed to have been that person.

This was above all true of his dreams of Sara Hutchinson. She was always in his heart during his waking hours; daytime events, tangling themselves onto the ever-winding thread of his feelings for her, would then scatter out into his dreams, which would thus tell him of her though they were not about her. Sometimes at the end of these confused dreams of meaningless events, the inspiration behind them would shine through, and Sara herself would appear with an incandescence of happiness that gave Coleridge one of his rare "sweet sleeps". More often it was only at the instant of waking that he recognized his dream as a symbol of Sara. These were the fortunate nights; there were others when the beings who stood for Sara would fade away and the dream would modulate into horror. "Mem. To examine whether Dreams of Terror and obscure Forms, ugly or not, be commonly preceded by Forms of Awe and Admiration with distant love" he wrote in his journal after the dream about Lady Sidney had faded into the nightmare of the vicious hags in the dark passage.

But though he could later examine such a dream with cool scientific curiosity as an example of the mechanisms of sub-conscious transitions, his first reaction to it was a scream of terror. Those night-shrieks of his had penetrated to every corner of the Coleridges' spacious house at Keswick; they must have been terrifying indeed for the other two passengers shut up with him in the cramped little cabin of the *Speedwell*.

VII · *Thursday 12th April*

"Why aren't you here?" wrote Coleridge in his notebook after a morning on deck in what seemed to him delightful weather, though *Leviathan*'s log mentions cloud and rain, light breezes and occasional squalls. The wind, veering between north-east and south-east, had carried the convoy into the Bay of Biscay, and Coleridge already recognized the caress of the south meeting them. Fresh as the breeze was, he felt the air was warmer and more genial, and the sky more blue. The *Speedwell* was rolling less, the sails of the convoy embroidered the horizon all around her, and the ever-changing pattern of the waves mesmerized his eye. It was all beauty and joy, but for that haunting question.

"Why aren't you here? This for ever. I have no rooted thorough thro' feeling—and never exist wholly present to any Sight, to any Sound, to any Emotion, to any series of Thoughts received or produced, always a feeling of yearning, that at times passes into Sickness of Heart". Whether he was looking at the rippling sea today, or brooding years earlier over the soft pulsing of a moorland well, the cry was still the same—"Why aren't you here?"

"You" was Sara Hutchinson. Coleridge first met her in 1799 at her brother's farmhouse at Sockburn on the banks of the Tees. She was the sixth of ten orphans, a strongly united family with many clannish jokes and habits and ways of doing things. Sara moved about between her brothers' farms, keeping house now for one, now for another. Coleridge fell in love with her almost immediately after their first meeting. The date and the occasion engraved themselves on his memory, and their anniversary was recorded with emotion in the journals of many subsequent years. The company on that November Sunday, which included some of Sara's brothers and her sister Mary—then not yet engaged to Wordsworth—was standing round the fire, talking, laughing, telling stories, asking riddles. Coleridge managed to hold Sara's hand in a long close clasp behind her back, "and then, then, for the first time love pricked me with his dart, poisoned, alas! and without remedy".

Sara Hutchinson was a very small woman, barely over five feet tall. Coleridge's daughter said she had a dumpy ungraceful figure, but Coleridge's children, who were fond of their mother, were not the most impartial witnesses about her rival. Sara seems to have been pleasingly plump, with a fine bosom which aroused some of Coleridge's most passionate feelings. Her other beauty was her hair, long, profuse, and in colour a shining brown. Her complexion was fair and she had a small head with a high forehead and a straight nose, judging by the only surviving picture of her, a silhouette; but none of those who described her appearance mentioned her features, and even Coleridge often had difficulty in visualizing her face when she was absent, hard as he tried, so there cannot have been anything notable about the outlines of her face. She said of herself later that she had never been a beauty, and presently she lost her teeth and became nutcrackerish and old-looking for her age, so that people meeting her for the first time thought her rather repulsive; but in 1804 when she was still under thirty she had the sturdy sleek attraction of some compact little animal like a squirrel, that one would want to stroke.

Between 1799 and 1804 Coleridge saw Sara at intervals when she stayed with the Wordsworths or he stayed with her and her brother. At first he persuaded himself that he could simply enjoy her company, their walks and talks and readings together, that it was possible for an unhappily married man to have a "virtuous and tender and brotherly friendship with an amiable woman". The lyrics which he wrote at this time about his love for her tended to be wish-fulfilment fantasies ending in the maiden confessing her love and falling into her lover's arms. But he could not be content for long in this unreal world of sentiment. He had a great moment of truth when he wrote the original *Dejection* in the form of a letter to Sara, admitting that his happiness was gone and that he was ruining hers too. He believed that they were meant to be a joy to each other, but there was nothing but sorrow for their love to expect, no way out, because his marriage was indissoluble—he considered that divorce was not permissible. He did confide to his notebook a hope that Sara might live with him without marriage, on some legally-guaranteed basis of permanency, but there is no evidence that he put the proposition to her. Nor is there any telling whether they ever consummated their love. Coleridge maintained that he remained faithful to his wife, and most of his biographers doubt whether he and Sara went beyond kisses and caresses. Coleridge certainly desired more; what Sara desired, or would permit, remains a mystery.

They had happy hours of companionship, and in his hopeful mood Coleridge could believe that she would love him for ever, sickly as he was and ugly as he thought himself. But there were many times of misery, when they were apart, when he was worrying about her health, or suspicious that she did not really love him as he loved her, or even resentful of the love which had brought him unhappiness and domestic strife, so that he longed for an "unencumbered heart" and to be alone with his books and his thoughts. By the autumn of 1803 he reached some kind of resolution that he must renounce Sara, and this strengthened his intention to go abroad, in hope of cutting the link. Sara seems to have encouraged this resolution, with more conviction than was welcome to Coleridge; he said of a letter of hers about this, which reached him in London a few weeks before he left, that it was "heart-wringing" and made him despair.

Was Coleridge's love for Sara Hutchinson a figment of his imagination or a real passion for a real woman? Many people, in his own day and since, have believed it was the former—not without support from Coleridge himself, specially when he was writing to his wife or her relations. "That to be in love is simply to confine the feelings prospective of animal enjoyment to one woman is a gross mistake—it is to associate a large proportion of all our obscure feelings with a real form" he told Southey. William and Dorothy Wordsworth came to believe that Coleridge's love for Sara was no more than a "fanciful dream", that his high-wrought emotions and ideals needed some focus, and merely happened to find this in Sara because she came in his way. Many of his recent biographers— quoting his fatally revealing admission "To be beloved is all I need" but not the following line, "And when I love, I love indeed"—have suggested that he felt no strong love for any of those near to him, though he demanded so much devotion and sympathy from them. Sara was not a real person in her own right for Coleridge, this theory runs; on the imaginative level she was his bright-eyed forget-me-not image of hope, his cryptogram for the ideal of love which existed only in his intellect; on the physical level she was a useful amanuensis and sick-nurse, and could be expected to provide admiration, playfulness and a few caresses by the evening fireside after he had worked all day at his writing. Other critics have suggested that his feeling for Sara was a substitute for religious devotion, a search for mystical experience.

For a mind like Coleridge's, the distinction between a real and an imaginary passion can hardly be drawn. No one who reads his note-books can doubt that he felt actual desire for Sara, a sexual urge and ache, a longing to lie with his cheek on her beautiful breasts. He or others have blotted out many phrases referring to her in his note-books, and Mary Wordsworth burnt most of his letters to Sara after her death. The ones that survive have occasional words of love and tenderness—"my Darling", "my best love", no more; but what has escaped obliteration in the notebooks is evidence enough of his feelings.

But it was his imaginative life that was the most real part of him, and Sara was intensely present in that. She was a part of all that he felt, her image lived within his most precious moments of vision, of enjoying natural beauty. He was to say at last, just before he finally lost her, "To bid me not love you were to bid me annihilate myself, for to love you is all I know of my life as far as my life is an object of my consciousness or my free will".

Nevertheless it is perhaps true that what Coleridge needed most of all, more than a wife or a mistress, was a sister. If he had had a congenial sister of his own, or if Dorothy Wordsworth or Sara Hutchinson—or even Mary Morgan or Lady Beaumont—had been his sister by blood, sharing his home and giving him companionship and sympathy, he might have been a safe and happy man. The possession of such a sister was one of the strongest motives for his complex jealousy of Wordsworth's domestic happiness.

Sara Hutchinson too might have liked best to have been Coleridge's sister. Her outstanding excellence was as a sister and friend. She was an ever-welcome guest in the houses of a whole circle of brothers, sisters, cousins, "each wishing to keep her longer, for she was a comfort and a blessing to them all" said Southey, who regarded her as one of his dearest friends. She was efficient, cheerful, level-headed, but also affectionate and long-suffering; Coleridge remem-bered in his old age how she would let the Wordsworth children tug and pull down her lovely hair. She was intelligent, too, and could discuss poetry with discrimination, sturdily maintaining her own opinion and her own choice; she made her own anthology from Coleridge's poems, mostly the light-hearted and joke ones. She was a maker of fun wherever she went, and her laughter spared nobody. It may be that she would have preferred to feel for Coleridge only the steady warm affection which she felt for her siblings and for Wordsworth. She deeply admired her brother-in-law and she was very fond of him, and was always willing to copy and discuss his poems—and also to criticize them if she did not like them. There has perhaps been some exaggeration about the adulation from his "harem" which surrounded Wordsworth. His wife, sister and sister-in-law revered and loved him, but they quite often twitted and jeered at him too. Sara at any rate kept her balance. But some of his poems seemed to tell her truths about herself. She was specially fond of his sonnet "Methought I saw the footstep of a throne"; perhaps she saw herself as the woman sleeping alone in a mossy cave with a smile of pleasant memories on her face? With a temperate balancing of advantage and disadvantage, she came down on the side of peace as against excitement in life. Later in her life she told someone of a younger generation that "Old Maid as I am, don't think that, though I firmly believe the balance of *comfort* is on our side, I am a favorer of a single life—comfort is but a meagre thing after all—but I have seen such misery in the marriage life as would *appal* you if you had seen it. Such millstones about the necks of worthy men! . . . Of course you will not suppose that I think all the fault belongs to the woman". She was repelled by demonstrative emotion, whether it was the outbreaks of a jealous wife or the hyperboles of an insistent lover. She did not care for being called an angel, she did not want to sit motionless gazing into Coleridge's eyes. She was a sensible lively four-square little woman who wore unstylish pea-green or lilac bonnets and unbecoming caps, and altogether seems to have strayed from the pages of Jane Austen into a group of people by a quite different author.

Coleridge and his son Hartley, reading their own natures into hers, called her "feeble in hope", "naturally despondent", but no one else saw this in her. Plenty of her own letters are extant, and they are shrewd, observant, readable, astringent—one can see why she would be fun to have in the house, and a good friend. But there is not a spark of imagination in them, even less than there is in the querulous but not unintelligent letters of poor Mrs Coleridge. Coleridge described Sara as having both sense and sensibility, but she is entirely an Elinor Dashwood, with nothing of Marianne. One can no more deduce from her cheerful unrevealing letters whether or not she felt any passionate love for Coleridge than one can deduce from Jane Austen's equally uncommunicative ones (those that her sister Cassandra did not destroy) whether or not she really loved and lost that legendary Devonshire suitor.

An attempt (in which Coleridge himself plays an enigmatic part) has been made to work up an alternative romance for Sara Hutchinson. There is said to be a tradition in the Wordsworth family that John Wordsworth, brother of William and Dorothy, who was a captain in the merchant navy and was drowned when his ship was wrecked in 1805, was engaged to Sara, or wanted to marry her, or his brother, sister and sister-in-law wanted him to marry her. There is no evidence in favour of this in Sara's or the Wordsworths' letters, and a good deal tending to disprove it. When the news of John's death reached Grasmere, Wordsworth wrote to describe Dorothy's, Mary's and his own affliction, and added "Sarah Hutchinson for ever bless her! has done us much good"; he would hardly have described her only as a comforter of the others if she herself had been engaged to the dead man. None of his or Mary's letters about his brother mention that he was engaged to be married, or dwell on his loss as special to any one member of that tightly knit circle. Sara's own letters of this time describe the sorrow of the Grasmere household with sympathy but with no tinge of personal grief.

The only positive statements come from Coleridge. Up to the time that he heard the news of John Wordsworth's death, there is no suggestion in his notebooks or letters that he knew John Wordsworth and Sara Hutchinson to be fond of each other, let alone engaged to be married; no sign of the jealousy of a rival lover which he felt in another and much less probable quarter. Yet when he heard the news of John's death he dashed down into his journal one of his most histrionic passages: "O William, O Dorothy, Dorothy!—Mary —and you loved him so!—and O blessed Sara, you whom in my imagination at one time I so often connected with him, by an effort of agonizing Virtue, willing it with cold sweat-drops on my Brow!" Three years later the story had hardened in Coleridge's imagination, and he told a friend outside the Wordsworth circle that if John Wordsworth had lived, Sara would have married him.

It seems quite possible that Coleridge invented the whole thing. Since Sara was out of his own reach, it was obviously less painful to imagine her vowed to a dead man than inclined to a living one. There is some evidence that John Wordsworth was in fact originally in love with *Mary* Hutchinson, not with Sara, but resigned his hopes when he realized that his brother William also loved her. It is equally possible that no passionate love was felt by any of those involved. The relationships between this group of people, so strong in their feelings, were complex but not necessarily sexual. Friendship, ardent but not physical, was a characteristic excellence of the nineteenth century. Many twentieth-century biographers are misled, when they read of endearments and caresses which today would inevitably have a sexual connotation, into detecting amours—even incest or homosexual love—in what was solely friendship or family regard. Of course there were cases, like Byron and Augusta Leigh or the Ladies of Llangollen, where more than friendships were involved. But strong and lasting attachments, without sexual content, between siblings, between man and woman, between man and man, between woman and woman, were perhaps the happiest human relationships in nineteenth-century England. English men and women in this period were not—with some notable exceptions— outstandingly gifted at marriage; extra-marital sex was often surrounded by prurience and hypocrisy; the parent-child relationship could be most unhappy; but affection between siblings and between friends was the mainstay of many lives. Not to understand this is a failure in historical imagination which has caused much nonsense to be written about William and Dorothy Wordsworth, about the Lambs, about the Brontës, about Elizabeth Barrett and her brother, and many others.

Coleridge, alone of the Grasmere circle, had never been blessed with a good sibling relationship. He envied Wordsworth for having such a sister and such a sister-in-law, but he could not altogether understand or believe in a relationship which he himself had never enjoyed, and suspicion sometimes climbed on the back of envy.

On this Thursday evening he was on the deck of the *Speedwell* after dark. The clouds had cleared, and the sky above the topmast was full of stars, whose reflections made dim pathways of light on the sea. Shimmers from the helmsman's lantern patterned the sails. Coleridge felt sick at heart, as lonely as his Mariner. His longing for Sara grew bitter with suspicion. That night he made a cipher entry in his notebook—

"Sickly thoughts about Mary dead and William married to Sara".

Coleridge's occasional fears that Wordsworth and Sara were in love with each other were baseless, and he generally recognized this in the long intervals between his paroxysms of suspicion. Only a week earlier he had been writing to the Wordsworths "O dear dear friends! I love you, even to anguish love you", and speaking of Wordsworth himself as "dearest and most revered William", "the man, for whom I must find another name than Friend, if I call any others but him by the name of Friend". The idea that if Mary died Wordsworth would then marry her sister was absurd; it would have been legally impossible, all else apart—marriage with a deceased wife's sister was then still forbidden. Coleridge could have been thinking of a liaison rather than marriage, but probability did not enter into it—he was overcome by a wave of morbid fear, impelled by his loneliness and his need of Sara, whose absence drained the life out of every beauty and joy. "Why aren't you here?"

Many years later he published a draft of a poem which was conceived about this period, to which he gave the beautiful name of *The Blossoming of the Solitary Date Tree*. A single date tree, he had read in Linnaeus, produces blossom but no fruit until a branch from another date tree is brought to it from far away. He lost the first stanzas of his poem as he originally wrote it, but he remembered that it was to have affirmed that

"What no one with us shares, seems scarce our own",

that only the presence of the best beloved gives meaning to the experience of beauty. "The finer the sense for the beautiful and the lovely, and the fairer and lovelier the object presented to the sense; the more exquisite the individual's capacity of joy, and the more ample his means and opportunities of enjoyment, the more heavily will he feel the ache of solitariness, the more insubstantial becomes the feast spread around him". In the surviving stanzas of the poem he imagined himself listening vainly for a voice—

"Beloved! 'tis not thine; thou art not there!"

VIII · *Friday 13th April*

Next day, when Coleridge in the *Speedwell* was crossing the Bay of Biscay, Dorothy Wordsworth at Grasmere was writing a letter to Lady Beaumont. It was a letter of thanks for a prosaic but welcome present of a cask of stout, which not only Wordsworth but the whole household would enjoy, Dorothy said. She had not yet met her correspondent, but she and Mary looked forward to getting to know her, and hoped she and her husband would come to Keswick again that summer, so that the Wordsworths could show them the countryside, including some of the "bye nooks unvisited by travellers".

An affection for Coleridge was one great link between Dorothy Wordsworth and Lady Beaumont, and Dorothy's letter was written partly to thank the Beaumonts for their kindness to Coleridge, and to give news of him, from the parting letters he had written to Wordsworth and to Southey. "I fear we shall not hear again", Dorothy went on, "for when he is in bad spirits he has not heart to write, and I dare not hope that he could be otherwise till he had lost sight of his native land, and found himself alone with his thoughts. Happily he has never yet been sea-sick, and the sea air agrees with him, so that, knowing the activity of his mind and its self-tranquil- lizing power in perfect solitude, we have no fears about his health during the voyage, and we try to console ourselves in the midst of regrets that we must for ever feel, with the hope that his long absence from his country and Friends will have a happy termination, and, indeed, with the melancholy certainty that if he had not gone, his life, for many years at least, must have been a life of sickness".

Dorothy had not had much leisure in the last few days before she wrote this letter. Wordsworth had been away from home for part of the time, visiting Sara Hutchinson and her brother Tom who had just moved into a new farm only a few miles away; and when he was at home he spent all his time in composing poetry, in a spate of inspiration. He was out of doors much of the time, gardening when he was not pacing up and down composing lines of poetry, but the weather was unkind; cold and gales had delayed the spring, and the trees were still leafless. The thresh of the wind in their bare branches, the rush of the water in the brimming roadside streams, wildly excited the Wordsworths' ten-months-old baby Johnny. Indoors he rampaged and demanded attention, and his doting aunt Dorothy gave it to him without stint. She had been ill in February, and had lost weight, but now she had sufficiently recovered her strength to be able to carry the heavy baby about for hours together. He was a strong vigorous handsome child, large for his age and much admired by all baby-fanciers. He could sit upright, and crawl a little, and his busy aunt occasionally got some leisure when he consented to remain on the floor and amuse himself. "He is far more happy in the day-time (except when he is sleepy or hungry) when we leave him to himself upon the carpet with good store of play-things than he is upon our knees. Give him but a work-basket full of tape and thread and other oddments and he riots among it like a little pussy-cat. He can sit upright upon the carpet and so we leave him—sometimes he gets a good bump upon his head and lustily he roars, but no matter, he cannot hurt himself seriously, so we are not afraid of him, and he will soon learn to take care of himself". But if Johnny was bored, he gave nobody any peace, but yelled so that he could be heard in every corner of the little house, until his mother or aunt took him up on her lap. The last part of Dorothy's letter to Lady Beaumont was written with Johnny on her knee, and she had to finish abruptly because Johnny demanded her attention and prevented her from writing.

The main care of the baby was in Dorothy's hands at this time because his mother, though she was still suckling him, was pregnant again and not in strong health. She had become very thin and looked so ill that her family were worried about her, and it had been decided that Johnny must be weaned. Coleridge's fears about Mary dying were not a mere by-product of his panic about Wordsworth and Sara; he had heard from Dorothy, just before his departure, about Mary's new pregnancy and the anxiety about her health. Mary Wordsworth, in every other way a noble character, pained her family by her almost wilful carelessness of her own health. She was so self-sacrificing that she could not see how anxious her family were about her.

Busy as they all were, the women of the Grasmere household had found time for another heavy task in the last few weeks. Coleridge had written in February to ask Mary and Dorothy to transcribe for him all Wordsworth's as yet unprinted poems. "Think what they will be to me in Sicily!" he implored; they would be a treasure, an inspiration, when he was far from his friends. The request was not a light one; it meant copying about eighty short poems, the *Duty* and *Immortality* odes, *The Ruined Cottage*, *Peter Bell*, and five books of what eventually became *The Prelude*. Dorothy and Mary, with some help from Sara Hutchinson, copied them all twice, because they wanted to keep corrected copies for themselves as well as sending a set to Coleridge; and all the time they were doing the copying, Wordsworth had to arrange and decipher his manuscripts for them so that they could get the order and text right. Wordsworth told Coleridge that it was very fortunate that he had been so insistent about having the poems, since although sorting and copying them had been an intricate and tiring job, it had secured the survival of a good deal of poetry which might otherwise have disappeared.

Hard as the work of copying had been, Dorothy was happy to think that the copies had reached Coleridge in time for him to take them with him on his voyage. "Thinking of his banishment, his loneliness, the long distance he will be from all the human beings that he loves, it is one of my greatest consolations that he has those poems with him". The copies reached Coleridge before he left London, occasioning a tremendous fuss and flurry of apologetic letters from Coleridge to John Rickman, Secretary to the Speaker of the House of Commons, under cover to whom they had been sent to avoid postage. Lady Beaumont saw that the manuscripts were safely stowed away in the travelling-desk which she gave Coleridge. It was late in the voyage before he looked at them.

Wordsworth would have been much upset if he had known this. He was longing to have Coleridge's opinion on the newest and most important part of the poetry copied for him, the opening books of what was eventually called *The Prelude*, but at this stage was thought of mainly as an introduction to *The Recluse*, and was known at Grasmere simply as "the poem to Coleridge". Wordsworth had been working on it vigorously in the last few months. Part of it was already in existence before Coleridge left Westmorland in January; Wordsworth read some of it aloud to him, high in the hills above Grasmere on a misty January morning, and Coleridge was much moved by this "divine Self-biography". The lines which Wordsworth read to him may have included the tribute to Coleridge himself, what he was and what he might become.

> "Fare thee well!
> Health and the quiet of a healthful mind
> Attend thee! seeking oft the haunts of men,
> And yet more often living with thyself,
> And for thyself, so haply shall thy days
> Be many, and a blessing to mankind".

By early March Wordsworth had reached the end of Book V of the "poem to Coleridge", and the whole work to that point was copied and sent to Coleridge. Much of the thought in it had been inspired by conversations with Coleridge, who had been urging Wordsworth for years to embark on a long poem on a grand scale. It was full of references to the beloved friend, the "brother of my soul" who had inspired it, and to have the judgement on it of that friend and brother was a burning wish of Wordsworth's. He told Coleridge in early March how anxious he was about this—his friend's help was important to him beyond words; and his farewell letter just before Coleridge set sail reiterated this wish still more strongly, specially as he had just heard of Coleridge's recent violent attack of cholera morbus. Wordsworth wrote that Coleridge's letter about that was "the severest shock to me, I think, I have ever received. I walked over for the Letter myself to Rydale and had a most affecting return home in thinking of you and your narrow escape. I will not speak of other thoughts that passed through me; but I cannot help saying that I would gladly have given three fourth of my possessions for your letter on The Recluse at that time. I cannot say what a load it would be to me, should I survive you and you die without this memorial left behind. Do for heaven's sake, put this out of the reach of accident immediately".

What can Coleridge—about to start on a dangerous voyage in poor health—have felt about the bleak implication that his closest friend would feel his death mainly because he had not produced comments on the friend's poetry before he died? Wordsworth did not mean it to sound like that, of course, but he never took any pains to appear amiable in his letters, he was always thinking of what he wanted to say, not of how it would sound. He was not going to speak of the other thoughts he had had about Coleridge as he walked home from Rydal, though if he had, they might have given Coleridge much-needed comfort. Both William's and Dorothy's letters to and about Coleridge at this time begin to show that lack of communication, that tinge of impatience, which at last, after many more years of forbearing friendship, were to end in lacerating separation. Dorothy, overburdened with household cares, had begun to find Coleridge too exigent and troublesome as a house-guest, too complaining and self-indulgent about his health. Wordsworth wrote to other friends about "poor Coleridge" and his miserable health.

But Wordsworth had proved his friendship in deeds if not in words by giving a promissory note for £100 to cover a loan to Coleridge for the expenses of his voyage, no mean gesture on the part of a man with a very small income and a growing family. And there was no lack of outspoken affection for him in the main part of

III   Ship of the Line Leaving Portsmouth. *Water-colour by J. M. W. Turner, 1828*

IV   "The Stars that start up, sparkle, dart flames and die away in the Snow of Foam by the vessel's side"; one of the sea patterns studied by Coleridge during his voyage

the joint farewell letter which the brother and sister wrote to Coleridge just before his departure. Dorothy assured him that their hearts were full of him, that they longed for his letters; she prayed for his health and peace of mind, and she ended "Farewell my beloved Coleridge, dear friend, Farewell! Believe me evermore, your faithful Friend". Wordsworth repeated Dorothy's entreaties that Coleridge would write at every opportunity, remembering how distressingly anxious for him his friends would be, and concluded "Heaven bless you for ever and ever. No words can express what I feel at this moment. Farewell farewell farewell".

Wordsworth had another way of making words express what he felt, a way which his natural reserve did not block as it did when he was writing letters. At the end of March he made an addition to the "poem to Coleridge", too late for it to be copied and sent to Coleridge before he left, though Dorothy told him of the existence of these new and "very affecting" lines, and wished that he could have taken them with him. They were the lines in Book VI about Wordsworth's and Coleridge's very different boyhoods, and Words-worth's wish that he could have known Coleridge then and con-soled his wretchedness, and about Wordsworth's admiration for his friend's learning and "gorgeous eloquence" and worship of beauty. No friend and poet could have speeded a parting poet friend with a more wonderful "bon voyage" wish than Wordsworth's—

"Far art thou wandered now in search of health
And milder breezes,—melancholy lot!
But thou art with us, with us in the past,
The present, with us in the times to come.
There is no grief, no sorrow, no despair,
No languor, no dejection, no dismay,
No absence scarcely can there be, for those
Who love as we do. Speed thee well! divide
Thy pleasures with us; thy returning strength,
Receive it daily as a joy of ours;
Share with us thy fresh spirits, whether gift
Of gales Etesian, or of loving thoughts".

E

IX · *Friday 13th April to Sunday 15th April*

The breeze that was carrying Coleridge on his way was not yet the northerly Etesian wind that Wordsworth invoked for him, but his convoy was making good progress. For Coleridge, when he came up on deck at nine o'clock on Friday morning, the wind was a brisk gale and the sea high, but *Leviathan*'s log reports only light south-easterly breezes, freshening later. The convoy was halfway across the Bay of Biscay, sixty-four leagues north-east of Cape Finisterre, and Coleridge learned from the *Speedwell*'s crew that if the present speed of six or seven knots was maintained all day, they would be opposite Bordeaux at eight o'clock that evening, and might see Cape Ortegal on the north coast of Spain next morning.

That afternoon at six o'clock the great guns of the *Leviathan* were fired as an exercise. Coleridge watched the smoke billowing upwards to form a beautifully-shaped cloud, which mingled with the masses of cumulus overhead. He longed for Sir George Beaumont to be there to paint the superb cloudscape. The *Speedwell* was the foremost ship in the convoy, even the *Leviathan* was slightly astern of her. The wind was dying; by half past seven there was almost a calm, and on one side of the *Speedwell* there was a clear sky and an empty sea, but on the other, half a mile away, was the towering *Leviathan* with the convoy around and behind her, under a magnificent canopy of white cloud, black-edged and streaked with the darkening gold of sunset. Between the *Speedwell*'s topmast and the horizon was the crescent moon with the old moon in her lap, and a bright planet glittering below her.

The *Speedwell* was the fastest merchant ship in the convoy, and was generally in the wake or abreast of the *Leviathan*, sometimes even ahead of her, never more than half a mile distant and sometimes only a furlong. Other ships in the convoy were less easy to handle, and the Commodore, Captain Bayntun, had a strenuous time keeping them together. The "Regulations and Instructions Relating to His Majesty's Service at Sea" laid down that a commodore in charge of a convoy "is to be careful in keeping the Merchant Ships all collected, and he is to be attentive, while he endeavours to proceed with all possible expedition, not to carry more sail than will admit of the heaviest sailing Ships keeping company with him, without risk of springing their Masts or straining the Ships". Some of the ships in the *Leviathan*'s convoy were always falling behind, and her log frequently records "Made and shortened sail as necessary", while the faster ships like the *Speedwell* were ordered to take in sails to wait for vessels astern. Every night, and sometimes during the day as well, the convoy hove to for two or three hours to wait for the laggards to catch up. "Every sail stretched, every rope in action; the sides of the vessel winged with Studding Sails, there he is, 2 leagues astern of the last of the Convoy, the Commodore of which is moving on, with half his masts bare—and he and the rest, what blessings they bestow on this Lag Sheep of the Flock!" noted Coleridge.

Occasionally if the laggards seemed to be making too little effort to keep up with the convoy, Captain Bayntun took more drastic action. The Regulations prescribed that "masters of merchant ships disobeying directions or not attending to signals or neglecting to carry a proper quantity of sail or by any other means retarding the progress of the Fleet" could be reported to the Admiralty; but the Admiralty was a long way off, and French warships or privateers might be a good deal nearer. Captain Bayntun's method of smartening up the laggards was more direct. "Fired a shot at the Neptune for not obeying the signal" reported *Leviathan*'s log. Coleridge, watching this operation from the *Speedwell* and gossiping about it with her crew, learned with amusement that such shots were known as "the Commodore's strengthening *Pills* for the Memory" and that the master of the merchant ship concerned was charged five shillings for the first shot, ten shillings for the next, and so on, doubling each time.

All Friday and Saturday Coleridge spent long hours on deck watching the ships, the movements of their sails, the guns being exercised, the manœuvres of the convoy. He saw it all with a curious detachment from the purpose and the dangers of the convoy's voyage. England was fighting for her life against a power that had dominated the Continent and threatened her with invasion, and the war at sea, of which this convoy was part, was the most active and vital sector of the war at this time. Coleridge had been a political commentator for London newspapers; he had at first sympathized strongly with France's revolutionary struggle, and had fiercely attacked Pitt's war policies; he now thought of Napoleon as a dangerous tyrant. But during this part of the voyage he seems almost to have forgotten that a war between England and France was in progress. The timeless irresponsible life of a passenger on board ship does seem often to produce this unnatural indifference. In June 1940 I sailed from Gibraltar to England in a convoy at a moment when the Germans had overrun Belgium, and France was capitulating; our convoy was thinly escorted and several ships in it were sunk by U-boats one moonlit night off Portugal; it seemed quite possible that the Germans would have landed in England before we got back there, if we survived to do so. But my diary of the voyage, though it does not totally ignore these great events as Coleridge's did, contains quite a lot of minor observation and gossip about personalities and shipboard life. One cannot be afraid twenty-four hours in twenty-four, or even consciously resolute and aware; one's mind persists in trivial routines and enjoyments throughout the most stirring events.

So Coleridge was able to gaze hour-long at the beautiful lines of the *Leviathan*, and watch the smoke of her guns floating upwards into exquisite cloud patterns, without giving a thought to the main purpose for which this magnificent object existed. He devoted pages of his notebook to an analysis of the shapes and symmetry which made up the picturesque effect of a warship: the proportions of hull to mast, of mast to sails, the bellying curves of canvas, the towering height of the topmast, the stream of the pennant, the latticed patterns of shrouds and ratlines, the shifting sunlight and cloud-shadows under which the sails showed sometimes snow-white, sometimes dingy, the fugitive suggestions of forms like towers or mountains or human figures as the complex pattern of sails and yards and booms dipped and swung to the Atlantic swell. The sensuous beauty perceived by his eye was enhanced by the intellectual apprehension that every part of this intricate pattern had "a strict and necessary action and reaction on all the rest, and that the whole is made up of parts, each part referring at once to each and to the whole, and nothing more administers to the Picturesque than this phantom of complete visual wholeness in an object, which visually does not form a whole, by the influence ab intra of the sense of its perfect Intellectual Beauty or Wholeness". He was never tired of watching the *Leviathan*; he saw her as a "majestic and beautiful Creature", seeming upright and motionless under her light spread of topsails, and yet gliding "as tho' its speed were spiritual—the being and essence without the body of motion, or as tho' the distance passed away by it, and the object of its pursuit hurried onward to it". And all around the convoy spread the sea-savannah, its unending vastness enhanced by the foreground of ships, its innumerable waves racing onwards to infinity with the sunshine glinting on their backs.

He wrote it all down in his notebook on deck, sitting on a coop full of ducks which quacked at his legs, and using the rudder case as a desk, or balancing his notebook on his knee. It was a small reddish-brown leather book, which could easily be slipped into a pocket. It opened upwards, like a stenographer's notebook, and Coleridge wrote across the upright pages with a pencil which was provided with the notebook, which he had bought in London in January. Its makers proudly boasted on the inside cover of the notebook that "The points on the pencils cannot break, and the writing is secure from erasure. Please to keep the point of the pencil smoothly scraped flat; then it may be held in the same direction as a pen, will always be in order, and the Metal, being about two inches in length, it will last a long time". This claim much annoyed Coleridge. "They begin to cheat with the metallic pencils" he wrote crossly in the notebook. "I am forced to take a new one from another Book, having completely worn out the one belonging to it; instead of being about 2 inches it was scarcely one; and the metal far softer and more wasteful".

He had intended these notebooks to be a record of the voyage for the benefit of the Wordsworths, but what he actually wrote in them was only partly a diary. Dated journal entries giving details of the weather, the progress of the voyage and his daily activities are interspersed with extracts from the books he was reading, memoranda of ideas and images for poems and essays, scraps of overheard dialogue, nautical terms and phrases, sketches and diagrams—and also prayers, appeals, laments, meant for no eye but his own.

Several entries show that if he grew tired of looking at the sea during these fine days, there were plenty of objects on the deck of the *Speedwell* to amuse his eye: a young lark, blown out to sea from the distant shore, which took refuge on board and was captured and soon revived to briskness; a dog, a cat with two kittens, the coops of ducks and chickens destined to figure on the ship's menu, three pigs in one of the boats, and a sheep in a pen with which Coleridge identified himself in one of his flashes of sympathy. He imagined it as coming from a countryside of flat peaceable meadows, and when he saw it cheerfully eating hay, he pictured its sensations, taking the brightness and sweet murmur of the sea for "dewy grass in sunshine, and the murmur of its trees". But next day, when a rough sea was throwing it about, "kneeling its poor face to the Deck, its knees black, worn and sore—up it starts, a great wave rushing over the ship—and staggers—and trembles under the Boat". If it had come from the rugged north country instead of the flat southern meadows, the storm would have been less terrible to it—a speculation which perhaps had a personal application for the Devonshire-born Coleridge who had come to grief among the Westmorland mountains.

He was thinking of northern hills and lakes when he was on deck late on Saturday evening, about eight o'clock. They had not made the expected progress, and were still in the Bay of Biscay, thirty-six leagues from Cape Finisterre and about level with Bordeaux, where they had hoped to be twenty-four hours earlier. The wind was south-easterly, and there had been intermittent squalls and drizzle that afternoon, so that the sky was piled with clouds. To Coleridge the cloud shapes at first looked like obelisks and turrets, or airy fleets of sailing ships, but presently he began to discern outlines of mountain scenery such as he had seen in Scotland or in Westmorland. The expanse of sea became a lake, and the black storm behind it a mountain ridge; it was as if he were walking among the hills of home, the landscape that he loved best.

While Coleridge scrutinized with uplifted heart this familiar out-line, Captain Findlay regarded it with foreboding as he paced up and down the deck, and gave orders to shorten sail, as the black cloud seemed to him to have a tempest within it. For the moment there was a lull, with heavy rain falling, and an uneasy swell thump-ing the *Speedwell*'s stern. The mate was aloft, whistling for a wind. "What a sweet Image to precede a Ship-wreck!" wrote Coleridge with airy confidence.

Captain Findlay's weather eye had not deceived him. From Saturday night to Monday morning they had a brisk squally gale from the east, with driving rain, and the *Speedwell* rolled so much that Coleridge, though not seasick, was knocked about by the blows of the sea on the hull and could not sit or stand with any comfort, so he stayed in bed. His bunk was not luxurious; it was made of boards, had a single hard mattress, and was only five feet ten inches long, almost exactly Coleridge's own height, and only twenty inches wide, though it was against the porthole, which gave him a bit more room. It was framed by Doric columns of wood, and had curtains flowered in yellow and brown. Coleridge was very well satisfied with it— "the best possible sitting, eating, drinking, writing, even shaving, mantel, it fails only in its original purpose, that of lying and sleep-ing; like a great Genius apprenticed to a wrong Trade", he good-humouredly commented. He had arranged his possessions very snugly by making a sort of shelf in the bottom half of the porthole opening, balancing a brown-paper parcel of books on a criss-cross of cordage, and piling on that his shaving-kit, teacup, soup plate, lemonade glass, inkstand and books. His dexterous contrivance seems to have impressed his shipmates; one of them described him as "a neat handed Fellow who could shave himself in a storm without drawing blood". But he was not always so handy when taking his early morning ginger tea; a rueful note reports "How at sea to indulge yourself with breakfasting in bed—and how in too great confidence of the Port Hole or carelessness, to scald below the hips".

The ship rolled comfortlessly all through Sunday night, as the convoy drove south, and Coleridge got little sleep. They had rounded Cape Finisterre on Sunday, and just before nine o'clock on Monday morning Coleridge heard the Captain on deck talking of Oporto, so he hurried up on deck, wrapped in a greatcoat and with bare feet. Fishing-boats were all round them, and the coast of Portugal, an outline of rolling mountains, was visible to the east. It was the first sight of land since the previous Wednesday.

X · *Monday 16th April to Wednesday 18th April*

All that Monday morning the convoy ran close under the Portuguese shore in brilliant sunshine. Leaning on the nettings along the side of the ship, Coleridge watched the fishing-boats with their ochre brown sails, and the fishermen in red or olive caps. Behind them stretched the glowing sea—"richest Green—I had seen nothing like it hitherto, nothing so green, no green so bright and rich—and violet purple, equal in light and richness: the violet purple now in large and small islands among the Green, now almost halving the field of Vision, and their Colors forming two seas, each a Shore to the other—now the Violet Purple running up into the Green, and vice versa in long Stripes, Coves, Spearheads and Tongues". Along the horizon spread the yellow-green Portuguese mountains, with dark cloud shadows moving across their broad shoulders, and with blue pyramids and cones of higher mountains rising behind them. The soft richness of colour all round him made Coleridge again long for his friend Sir George Beaumont to be there to paint it.

Before noon they were off Oporto, and seven of the merchant ships parted from the convoy to run into the port. Coleridge peered through a telescope at the sprawling city, which looked to him as burnt and clayey as a vast brick kiln, or perhaps it was more like a ruined city in a wilderness. The country round it was darkly wooded, behind it rose a circle of peaks and saddlebacks, and the sea between it and the ship was coloured a delicious golden green by the outflowing water of the river Douro. The air was balmy with a springlike warmth tempered by the fresh sea breeze. Coleridge was filled with well-being as the convoy bore off from the land again, and sailed south. They passed Cape Mondego, "a bold Ness of deepest purple Blue", in the afternoon. The sun was so hot that the *Leviathan* loosed her small sails to dry, and Coleridge went to sleep on the bare deck in the golden afternoon.

But that night was squally and rainy again, and the *Speedwell* rolled wretchedly. "This damned rocking depresses me inconceivably—like Hiccups or Itching, it is troublesome and impertinent and forces you away from your Thoughts—like the presence and gossip of an old Aunt or long staying Visitor to two Lovers". He had a night of bad dreams which made him weep in his sleep and wake to find his pillow wet with tears. He dreamt of old and recent friends, and yet the dream was not about them, they did not appear, the beings in his dreams were quite unlike them, yet he recognized them. It was all mixed up with his own schooldays, and it was pity for the unhappy boy that he had been fifteen years ago that made him weep in his dream.

The convoy passed Berlenga Island at daybreak on Tuesday, and Capa da Roca at noon. The wind was now north-westerly, and the rain stopped in the afternoon as they came in sight of Lisbon. The convoy hove to while four more of its ships parted company and sailed into Lisbon. Coleridge was on deck scrutinizing the coastline, the yellow beach below the Rock of Lisbon and the bold outline of the ridge running up from it, a "wild striding Edge" which he tried to draw, and a village which he thought was Cintra, and a distant prospect of breast-shaped and domed mountains, with what looked like palaces and convents on their slopes.

His health had deteriorated in the last thirty-six hours, with stomach and bowel trouble, a painful boil, and his left eyelid swollen and red. But on Wednesday morning, after another night of bad dreams, he felt a pleasurable sleepiness and a return of well-being, which he increased by a drastic salt-water purge, and that day he was able to eat a better dinner than he had managed for the last six weeks, though he was still eating no meat or fish or poultry.

Dinner in the *Speedwell* was always at one o'clock, and was in the cabin, where Captain Findlay, Coleridge and the other two passengers sat down to the main meal of the day. For anyone feeling at all queasy, the two other passengers were trying companions at table. Hastings, the merchant, was sensual and greedy, "not deficient in sense or judgement, but inert to every thing except Gain and eating". He informed Coleridge four or five times that good wine never did any man any harm, though it was clear to Coleridge from his suffused complexion that half his liver was gone or going. As for the fat Mrs Ireland, her conversation was entirely and lovingly devoted to food. "O Christ! for a seasick man to see the man eat, and this Mrs Carnosity talk about it" Coleridge groaned. Mrs Ireland earned a fine burst of vituperation in his notebook and letters. She had a horrible superfluity of flabby flesh, and her mind was un-utterably feeble, though she had travelled all over the world and met all sorts of people. All her experiences, speculations, pleasures, were concentrated on food. Her expectations of her destination at the end of this voyage were confined to what she would eat when she got there: "I don't know what I shall say to the Apricot Tarts at Malta". There was something almost poetic in the gusto with which she discussed food. Coleridge made a verbatim report of some of her remarks, which clearly fascinated him by their sheer abysmal triviality. "She eats everything by a choice. 'I must have that little potatoe' (baked in grease under the meat) 'it looks so smilingly at one'. 'Do cut me if you please' (for she is so fat, she cannot help herself) 'that small bit—just there, Sir!—a leettle bit *below*, if you please'. 'Well! I have brought plenty of pickles, I *always* think, etc.'

'I have always three or four jars of brandy cherries with me; for with boiled rice now etc for I always think etc'—and true enough, if it can be called thinking, she does always think upon some little damned article of eating that belongs to the Housekeeper's Cupboards and Locker".

All day she was eating, drinking, or yawning—plaintive crying yawns something between a moan and the whimper of a spoilt child trying to cry. She confided to Coleridge that she always thought how unhappy one always was if there was nobody and nothing to amuse one, it made one so nervous. The idea of this mountainous woman—whose mind was totally vacant, who snored all night and ate all day—being nervous exasperated Coleridge, who reckoned he knew what it was to be really nervous. But Mrs Ireland was too stupid and good-natured to have any idea of the impression she was making, and she drivelled happily on and on about her determination to bring with her enough of various forms of food—"I always think them is comfortable". There is a certain sublimity about her single-mindedness. The family of General Fox, to whom she had been housekeeper, must have been uncommonly well fed. She was certainly the right type of oddity to appeal to Southey, to whom Coleridge's description of "Mrs Carnosity" was sent. The panorama of the Portuguese mountains and cities in the last few days had ensured that the first letter home which he wrote would be to Southey, a lifelong devotee of Portugal. "I need not say, that the Sight of the Coast of Portugal made it impossible for me to write to anyone before I had written to you, I now seeing for the first time a country, you love so dearly".

XI · *Monday 16th April*

When Coleridge started his letter to Southey on 16th April, he expressed the hope that the Southeys' baby might already have been safely born, that it was a boy, and that Southey was by now in London.

But on this Monday, Southey was still in Keswick. Edith Southey had not yet had her baby, and Southey—unlike Coleridge, who had managed to be away from home when two of his three children were born—was too kind a husband to leave home at such a time, specially as in the previous summer the Southeys had lost their first child. Coleridge knew how anxious Southey was, and in his previous letter had expressed his sympathy, with the effusiveness which was apt to set Southey's teeth on edge. "I have said nothing of Edith; but that which you let no one know of in the bottom of your Heart, that same anxiety and hope and fear flutters at the bottom of mine".

Southey needed to get to London, to do the research for an anthology on which he was working. He could not afford to neglect any pot-boiling commissions, as he had to support his own family entirely by his pen, and it was beginning to look as if he might have to support Coleridge's as well. He worked exceedingly hard, taking on a quantity of book-reviewing as well as the revision of his long poem *Madoc* and the everlasting labour on his *History of Portugal*. He roused the Keswick household for breakfast every day with a boatswain's call, and then had to shut himself up in his study from breakfast to dinner, from dinner to tea, and from tea to supper, only occasionally emerging to play with the children or his dog, or to get a breath of air throwing stones in the river at the bottom of the orchard. His books were his real companions, the only but sufficient intellectual equals among those with whom his days were passed. "In plain truth, I exist more among the dead than the living, and think more about them, and perhaps feel more about them" he confessed to Coleridge, who told him that his library was his real wife.

Southey's study at this time was barely furnished with two chairs and a table, roughly plastered with the ceiling criss-crossed with the lines of the plasterer's trowel, and bitterly cold and draughty; it was so large that Southey felt like "a cock-robin in a church" as he sat working there in his old black coat and corduroys, with a green shade to protect his eyes. But the walls were lined with his treasured library, and beyond the windows there was a delectable view of mountains and lakes, so that Southey likened his icy laborious days to purgatory, "a state of torment with heaven in view". Greta Hall, where the Coleridges had lived since 1800, stood on a hill on the outskirts of Keswick, with Skiddaw behind, the horseshoe-curved river Greta in front, and Bassenthwaite and Derwent Water stretching away among the hills. Southey and his wife had arrived in Keswick seven months earlier to stay with the Coleridges, so that Mrs Southey could have the consolations of her sister Mrs Coleridge in her grief at the death of her little daughter Margaret. They had fitted smoothly enough into the household which was to be their lifelong home. Coleridge was thankful to have them there, it made his departure abroad much easier. "Your presence at Keswick is beyond all Compare my greatest *Comfort*" he told Southey.

Southey was saddened by Coleridge's departure, for selfish and unselfish reasons. He already suspected that he might be left holding the baby, but that was not the whole story. He missed Coleridge's companionship, "in almost all moods of mind, for all kinds of wisdom, and all kinds of nonsense". Like Wordsworth, he treasured Coleridge's literary advice; describing his project for an anthology to Coleridge, he added "how much the worse it will be for your voyage to Malta, few but myself will feel". Although the project for Coleridge's going abroad had been in the air for so long, Southey had doubted whether it would ever really come off, and when Coleridge actually went south to London and booked his passage, the shock of imminent separation surprised Southey into more warmth and open affection than his letters usually showed. "God grant you a speedy passage, a speedy recovery, and a speedy return! I will write regularly and often" he promised, and two days later he wrote again that " your departure hangs upon me with something the same effect that the heavy atmosphere presses upon you—an unpleasant thought, that works like yeast, and makes me feel the animal functions going on", and he ended

> "God bless you! prays your
> Old friend and brother
> R. Southey".

Monday 16th April

The two men had once been estranged, after their enthusiastic friendship on first meeting; they were now again on amicable terms, but far apart intellectually, and critical of each other; yet there was something between them, limited but firm, which gave Coleridge more of a feeling of security, though infinitely less excitement, than his friendship with Wordsworth.

Southey's opinion of Coleridge was a mixture of reverence and exasperation. He considered Coleridge's intellect as the finest he had ever encountered; all other men were as children in comparison with him; his mind was "infinitely and ten-thousand-thousand-fold the mightiest of his generation". But no one would believe this when he was dead, because he wasted all his huge powers by his want of resolution. In the fortnight before Coleridge left for Malta, Southey wrote pen-portraits of him to two friends, which tell one a good deal about Southey's own character as well as about Coleridge's. To John Rickman, who had been meeting Coleridge in London and had not been favourably impressed, Southey wrote "you are in a great measure right about Coleridge; he is worse in body than you seem to believe, but the main cause lies in his own management of himself, or rather want of management. His mind is in a perpetual St Vitus's dance—eternal activity without action. At times he feels mortified that he should have done so little; but this feeling never produces any exertion. I will begin tomorrow, he says, and thus he has been all his life-long, letting today slip. He has had no heavy calamities in life, and so contrives to be miserable about trifles. Poor fellow! there is no one thing which gives me so much pain as the witnessing such a waste of unequalled power . . . Having so much to do, so many errors to weed out of the world which he is capable of eradicating, if he does die without doing his work, it would half break my heart, for no human being has had more talents allotted".

If only Southey himself had had the luck to be allotted such talents, what a use *he* would have made of them; the unspoken envy is evident. Nevertheless the summing-up is neither unfair nor quite unsympathetic. Four days later, writing to a woman friend, Southey showed more affection and more self-knowledge in his description of his friend. "Coleridge is gone for Malta, and his departure affects me more than I let be seen. Let what will trouble me, I bear a calm face; and if the Boiling Well could be drawn (which, however it heaves and is agitated below, presents a smooth, undisturbed surface), that should be my emblem. It is now almost ten years since he and I first met, in my rooms at Oxford, which meeting decided the destiny of us both; and now when, after so many ups and downs, I am, for a time, settled under his roof, he is driven abroad in search of health. Ill he is, certainly and sorely ill; yet I believe if his mind were as well regulated as mine, the body would be quite as manageable. I am perpetually pained and mortified by thinking what he ought to be, for mine is an eye of microscopic discernment for the faults of my friends; but the tidings of his death would come upon me more like a stroke of lightning than any evil I have ever yet endured; almost it would make me superstitious, for we were two ships that left port in company".

The last phrase was a quotation from a farewell letter which Coleridge had just written to him from Portsmouth. Coleridge's self-identification with a voyaging ship, implicit ever since the writing of *The Ancient Mariner*, came out into the open as he set out on his Malta voyage. The boiling well image in Southey's letter was borrowed from Coleridge too. Southey hoarded images, carefully listing them in notebooks; they did not swim up spontaneously to the surface of his imagination, as they did to Coleridge's.

Coleridge was as clear-sighted about Southey's limitations, and as generous about his merits, as Southey was to Coleridge's. He admitted and admired Southey's rectitude, purity, industry, regularity, his hatred of oppression and injustice, his kindness and liberality; he was a good husband, brother, father, master to his servants. But he had no warmth, no delicacy of feeling, no real self-knowledge; he could be spiteful and wounding from sheer lack of sensibility, he could not lose his own self-contained entity in an outgoing flood of emotion. Error aroused his indignation but not his pity. He had none of the "sea-like sound and motion" of love, he was a "clear handsome piece of Water in a Park".

XII · Monday 16th April

Southey's virtues and good looks, like Sir Charles Grandison's, seem to have irritated most people, then and now. But if one had been a deserted wife or an insecure child, Greta Hall under Southey's rule would have been a reassuring place to live. Coleridge's children loved and trusted Southey. He played games and went for picnics with them, told them fairy stories but bracingly ridiculed their fears of the dark, and allowed them into his study however busy he was. It was a good house for children, with plenty of rooms, including a large dark attic full of lumber where a bogey was believed by the children to lie in wait. The parlour window overlooked a horseshoe-shaped lawn surrounded by flower-beds, still dark brown and bare after the cold late spring. In front of the house, sloping down towards the town of Keswick and the bridge over the Greta, was a large nursery garden, and at the back there was an orchard of apple and plum trees, below which was a wood leading down to the river, with a path running along the bank. There was plenty of room for the children to play, and plenty of pets to play with: Southey's dog Dapper, "the veriest coward that ever carried a tail,—the very sucking pigs frighten him; but he is a good fellow for all that" said his indulgent master—and a whole succession of cats with fantastic names like Bona Fidelia or Ovid or Pope Joan. They were apt to take refuge in Southey's study, as the quietest place in a house full of children, and they were sure of a welcome there; Southey kept one hand free to play with the cat even when he was writing with the other.

The two women who shared the household ran it with a good deal of fuss and unpunctuality, but with certain standards of tidiness and regard for appearances, which contrasted with the austerity, the smoky disorderly rooms, the tattered books, the free roughness, of the Wordsworths' cottage at Grasmere, with young Johnny

Wordsworth yelling on the floor in a tangle of cotton-reels. Dorothy Wordsworth despised Mrs Coleridge for taking all morning to dress herself and her children, but they did eventually emerge looking neat and orderly. One is reminded of the "kind of slow bustle" in which Jane Austen's Mrs Price spent her days; and Mrs Coleridge resembled Mrs Price in another way. Mrs Price, Jane Austen tells us, would have been a happy and successful woman if she could have married someone like her sister's husband Sir Thomas Bertram; and Sarah Fricker would have had a different and happier life if she had married someone like her sister Edith's husband Southey, instead of marrying Coleridge. She would have preferred to marry Southey, and believed him to be fond of her, so his choice of her sister Edith had been a disappointment. But her passions were never at all strong, and any kind respectable hard-working husband would have done. If she could have married a worthy commonplace man, preferably living in Bristol where all her friends were, a man who earned a good living and got on well with other ordinary men, and was well thought of by them, she would have made an affectionate and happy wife to him. Coleridge could offer her none of this, and what he offered instead—genius, fitful literary success, an exiguous and uncertain income, brilliant talk, a lonely home among beautiful mountains—had no attractions for her.

Coleridge asked Sarah Fricker to marry him because he needed a wife for the Pantisocratic scheme of a colony in Pennsylvania, and Southey, who was the other prime mover in the scheme, had just got engaged to Sarah's sister. Coleridge very soon realized that he had mistaken his own feelings; indeed, he was really in love with another woman, Mary Evans, at the time; but she rejected him, and Southey made sure that Coleridge did not escape from his sister-in-law; she herself, or her sister, also did some arm-twisting by telling Coleridge that she had turned down two proposals, one of them from a rich man, for his sake, and that her uncle was persecuting her in consequence.

In spite of this unpromising start, the marriage was happy at first. Coleridge found his wife attractive and sexually satisfying, and when their children began to arrive she proved a good and devoted mother.

F

Monday 16th April

So long as they were living in Bristol or Nether Stowey, near Mrs Coleridge's own family and friends, and near Thomas Poole, the only one of Coleridge's own friends that she liked and trusted, all went fairly well. If she was jealous of the irruption of the Wordsworths into Coleridge's life at this time, the feeling was not strong enough to be a real danger to domestic harmony.

Disillusionment had set in with Coleridge by October 1799 when he wrote that "the wife of a man of Genius who sympathizes effectively with her Husband is a rara avis with me". A few days later he met Sara Hutchinson for the first time, and all chance that the reality of his marriage could endure was over.

He believed that marriage was indissoluble, not as "the effect of spells uttered by conjurors", but because permanent cohabitation was useful to the community as the best means of securing the nurture and education of children. He never contemplated divorce from his wife, and he seems to have remained technically faithful to her. But after the first few years of marriage she was sexually cold to him, and their minds and hearts grew further and further apart. She was not interested in his writing, of which she had a low opinion; she did not want to live in the country; she was worried by his illnesses and their poverty; and she was jealous of the Wordsworths and above all of Sara Hutchinson.

The marriage reached a crisis during the winter of 1801-2, and Coleridge contemplated a separation on the grounds of their total incompatibility. The threat of a separation frightened Mrs Coleridge into efforts for reconciliation, and Coleridge resolved that when he returned to Keswick from London they would "live together as affectionate Husband and Wife ought to do". By May she was pregnant again, and though Coleridge regarded this as regrettable, the summer of 1802 passed in comparative peace. But by the autumn they were quarrelling again; she was showing her jealousy of Sara Hutchinson, and he was defending his right to choose his own friends and, less reasonably, demanding that she should love them too. Their youngest child, yet another Sara, was born on 22nd December. For the next fifteen months, up to Coleridge's departure to Malta, he and his wife kept on some sort of terms; both of them were making an effort, and the children helped to hold them together. Love was altogether dead, and there were quarrels, but Coleridge still felt it was his duty to be her protector and friend, still assured her of his honour and virtue. His final letter to her from Portsmouth, just before he sailed for Malta, seems an expression of what he wished to feel, and thought would sound well, rather than a sincere and spontaneous goodbye message.

"My dear Sara! the mother, the attentive and excellent Mother of my children must needs be always more than the word friend can express when applied to a woman. I pray you, use no word that you use with reluctance. Yet what we have been to each other, our understandings will not permit our Hearts to forget!—God knows, I weep Tears of Blood, that so it is!—For I greatly esteem and honor you. Heaven knows, if I can leave you really comfortable in your circumstances, I shall meet Death with a face, which I feel at the moment I say it, it would rather shock than comfort you to hear".

The whole of this hollow letter must have given more shock than comfort to Mrs Coleridge. She was an insensitive woman, but not a stupid one. Coleridge himself said that she had "considerable intellect", and her own letters, though they are flat, common sense and without nuance, show a reasonable amount of observation, and sympathy with other people's concerns, and are sometimes quite vivid in description of men and events, though it is only the outsides of things and people that interest her. She was quite well educated, able to teach French and Italian, writing and arithmetic, to her own and the Southeys' children. She made a good impression on casual acquaintances, who found her affable, unaffected, good-natured and pleasant. Her appearance was decidedly prepossessing, and was enhanced by neat and becoming clothes. She was a short woman, pleasantly plump, with large dark eyes, heavy black eyebrows beneath a low forehead, an aquiline nose, full rather pouting lips, and an incipient double chin. She was prettier than Sara Hutchinson, and intellectually not much her inferior, but she was chilly and fretful where Sara was warm and composed. She did not stand much chance, and she threw away what chances she had.

But one thing she did not do, though it would have been in her power—she did not turn Coleridge's children against their father. All three grew up to admire and love him, though they saw very little of him all through their adolescence. If there had not been some real stuff in the marriage, the children would not have grown up loving both their parents long after the marriage had broken. Hartley's love for his mother in later years had a patronizing tinge; he spoke of her as "poor dear Mama", made fun of her "Job-ish" tendencies, and was loftily grateful for her supplies of money and clothes, her hints to him about the advisability of praising Uncle Southey's poetry; while her unnecessary humility over her position at Greta Hall as Southey's hanger-on offended him. But though he did not think much of her intelligence, he was fond of her and dependent on her love for him.

It was the younger Sara Coleridge who did the fullest justice to her mother, in a summing-up of her personality which is worthy of Coleridge's daughter for its penetration and brilliance, and is made utterly convincing by its note of exasperated affection. It was pro-voked by De Quincey's depreciating description of Mrs Coleridge's appearance and character in his *Recollections of the Lake Poets*, which Sara Coleridge considered unfair and impertinent. She knew that her mother could be a trial, deserving the name of "Frettikins" which her daughter sometimes gave her, not generally admired for goodness as Mrs Wordsworth was; but her character had a deep foundation of integrity which deserved reverence, not De Quincey's sneers. Sara Coleridge wrote a letter to her husband about her mother, which is the best and fairest epitaph for this much-discussed marriage.

"The impression which the account of my mother would have is that she is a mean-minded unamiable woman with some respectable qualities and that my father married from opportunity rather than much attraction of hers. My mother's respectability it did not rest with him to establish; her attractions he greatly under-rates and the better points of her temper and understanding are not apparent in his partial sketch. . . . The sort of wife to have lived harmoniously with my father need not have possessed high intellect or a perfect temper—but greater enthusiasm of temperament than my mother possessed. She never admires anything she doesn't understand. Some women, like Mrs Wilson and Mrs Wordsworth, see the skirts of a golden cloud—they have unmeasured faith in a sun of glory and sublime region stretching out far beyond their ken, and proud and happy to think that it belongs to them are ready to give all they have to give in return. This faith, this docility, is quite alien to the Fricker temperament . . . my mother's very honesty stood in her way—unless at the same time she had possessed that meekness and forbearance which softens everything and can be conciliating by utter silence on all unpeaceful topics and the constant recurrence to soothing cheering themes. Neither had my mother that dexterity in managing the tempers of others which is often a substitute for an even temper in the possessor. She has no power over her mind to keep the thought of petty cares and passing interests (the importance of which is often mere matter of fancy) in abeyance. She never compares on a wide scale the real importance of the thing with the degree of energy and time and vital spirit that she spends upon it; and though her talents are above mediocrity and her understanding clear and good—on its own range—she has no taste whatever for abstractions and formerly had less toleration for what she did not relish than now. But to say broadly or to imply unreservedly that she is harsh-tempered or narrow-minded (that is, of an ungenerous spirit) or more unintellectual than many women who have pleased my father is to misrepresent the subject. My father had a good opinion of her understanding, and a very high one of her personal attractions".

XIII · *Thursday 19th April*

The convoy rounded Cape St Vincent on the 18th, and with a fresh breeze sailed on south-east towards the Straits of Gibraltar. There was a bright moon that Wednesday night, which was not welcome to a commodore taking a convoy uncomfortably near to the French and Spanish ships in Cadiz; *Leviathan*'s log reported suspiciously "Two strange sail in sight". But to Coleridge the moonlight on the sea made a mysterious colour symphony for which he could not find the precise words. It was like an island of grey-white reeds on a tossing lake, it was like metal plating on green bottle-glass. His sentences tangled and broke as he tried to capture the exact impression.

On Thursday morning Cape Trafalgar was in sight. By ten o'clock Coleridge was sitting on the duck coop with his notebook on the rudder case, jotting down his impressions of the land now visible on each side—the distant African coast to his right, and on his left the Spanish coast running back to Cadiz, a perspective of mountain ridges like upturned canoes, with scars of light red clay on their dark brown crests. As the convoy moved on into the Straits, the Spanish coast grew more distinct. It was a desolate pile of stony mountains and plunging cliffs, with streaks of white rock glaring through the dark heath and brushwood on the slopes. The sunlight came and went; when a cloud crossed the sea, the sides of the waves shimmered like brass. On the African coast Apes Hill loomed up in the foreground with three or four mountains behind "like chimneys in the Clouds—and one old stooping Giant looking in upon us 20 leagues inland".

Coleridge said to himself "This is Spain!—That is Africa! Now, then, I have seen Africa!" and at first he did get a slight thrill and quickening of the pulse at the thought. But as soon as he started to analyse his sensations, he realized that the bare fact of such a new experience was not significant in itself, it amused the mind but did not exercise it or elevate it. It was not just because the old stooping giant of a mountain was in Africa that it moved him, it was for itself. "At the same time, and gradually winning on the other, the nameless silent Forms of Nature were working on me, like a tender Thought on a man, who is hailed merrily by some acquaintance in his work, and answers it in the same tone". Geographically, politically, there was sharp division between Europe on his left and Africa on his right, but the distinction was unreal; in Nature they were one, two banks of the noble sea stream. He went on to reflect how little the historical associations of places meant to him and to Wordsworth. Even Shakespeare's mulberry tree would mean more to him as a beautiful pattern of branches and roots than because it was Shakespeare's. Were there any places anywhere whose associations would make them more sacred to him, he wondered? Perhaps the rock on the sea shore where Giordano Bruno, fleeing from the pursuing Inquisitors, decided to return and witness to the truth; or the primrose bank where the young Milton used to lie in the dawn of his poetic inspiration; or the roadside from which Shakespeare caught his first view of London, and asked himself "And what am I to do there?" An unforced imaginative response of this kind to the moments that formed the lives of great minds was utterly different from the degrading routine of organized sight-seeing, as different as true enthusiastic religion was from the superstitious pilgrim's peering at the shin-bones in a saint's coffin. Was it the natural bent of the mass of mankind, or could one hope that it was only their faulty education, that made them feel pleasure only from what tickled their fancy, from "gratifications of curiosity, Novelty, Surprize, Wonderment from the Glaring, the harshly Contrasted, the Odd, the Accidental"? Coleridge's list sounds like the perfect recipe for increasing the circulation of a newspaper. If better education is the remedy, the century and a half since Coleridge made this prescription has not yet worked a cure.

It was lucky for the convoy that a favourable wind was carrying it rapidly towards Gibraltar. Coleridge had heard stories from Captain Findlay of what could happen to ships becalmed in the Straits.

Thursday 19th April

"We have a breeze that promises to let us laugh at Privateers and Corsairs that in a calm will run out, and pick up a Merchant Vessel under the very stern of the Commodore, as a Fox will a Fowl when the Wolf dog that guards the poultry yard, can only bark at him from his Chain". Coleridge had realized before he left England that one of the perils of the voyage would be the possibility of being taken prisoner by Algerine corsairs or French privateers. The piratical vessels which lay in wait in the Gut of Gibraltar were a notorious menace to British shipping. Nelson always referred to them as "row-boats", which now suggests a dinghy which one man can scull, but these were powerful heavily gunned galleys with dozens of rowers, faster than anything but a small sailing-ship with a fair wind behind her. They could easily sink a warship's boat; there was a story that one of them had nearly reduced a frigate to striking her colours. Then there was the French warship *L'Aigle* lurking in Cadiz harbour; unless passing convoys had an escort of a ship of the line which could take on *L'Aigle*, they were in danger of a sortie by her. Three British frigates under Captain Gore kept watch outside Cadiz, but they were not big enough to take on the French ship if she did come out; Gore was keen to try, but Nelson did not want him to risk it.

The protection of convoys going through the Straits of Gibraltar was one of Nelson's biggest anxieties at this time. His letters to the Admiralty and to the Fleet under his command are full of it. In December 1803 the Committee of Merchants Concerned in the Trade to Gibraltar and the Mediterranean complained to the Admiralty about the depredations on British shipping committed by "the French Row-boats that rendezvous at Tariffa and Ceuta", and the Admiralty passed on the complaint to Nelson, directing him to do something about it, and pointing out that "it is of great importance that some arrangement should be made for the protection of our Trade on its entering the Straits". Nelson replied with some irritation that he was perfectly aware of the dangers that merchant ships ran in the Straits from French row-boats and privateers, and that he had been taking measures against them for the last six months, stationing sloops in the Straits and ordering

Gore's squadron outside the Straits to destroy as many as possible of these boats "which infest that Coast, and from the Spanish ports commit the most unprincipled acts of piracy". He was doing all he could with the few ships at his disposal, he protested to the Admiralty. On the same day he wrote to the captains of the sloops *Halcyon* and *Weazle*, then based on Gibraltar to operate against the pirates, reminding them that "the most active service against the Enemy's Privateers in the Straits of Gibraltar, as well for the protection of our Trade and the comforts of the Garrison at that place, is expected of His Majesty's Sloop under your command". A few days later he was planning for eastbound Mediterranean convoys to pass north of Ibiza and Majorca, for fear of capture by the Algerines, unless they were escorted by a ship of the line. A fortnight before Coleridge's convoy sailed from Portsmouth, Nelson was issuing a whole batch of orders about convoys to his captains. The captain of the *Madras* was censured for having allowed a homeward-bound merchant ship to sail from Malta without convoy; the *Agincourt* was sent to Gibraltar to cruise outside the Straits to protect British shipping and attack enemy privateers, until further orders; the captain of the *Monmouth*, about to escort a convoy from Malta to Spithead, was ordered to proceed as fast as possible, consistently with safety, and to pay strict attention to keeping the convoy together and protecting them from the enemy; the *Argo* was to accompany the *Monmouth*, or to take the convoy instead if the *Monmouth* was not available, as "I consider the protection of our Trade the most essential service that can be performed". It was a brain-cracking task to work out what ships could be spared at the right time and place for this essential service, out of such a small and fully extended Fleet; and on 14th April, when Coleridge's convoy was only five days away from the Straits, Nelson was writing urgently to the Admiralty for an extra fast-sailing brig to be sent out to patrol the Gut of Gibraltar and protect shipping from the privateers, some of whose ships now had up to twenty-six guns, and crews of two hundred men.

But no privateer attacked Coleridge's convoy, now consisting of the *Leviathan* and twenty-five other ships. Captain Bayntun shepherded them into the Straits, firing a shot at one of the merchant ships in the convoy which had failed to obey his signal. The crew of the *Leviathan* was mustered by divisions, and everything made ready for the arrival at Gibraltar. Coleridge on the *Speedwell*'s deck was watching Europa Point, the first segment of the Rock of Gibraltar, sliding into view as they rounded Tarifa Point, whose green fields and clustered houses reminded him of Keswick, only that the houses were tiled instead of slated. In all these alien landscapes he tried to discern a link with home—the mountains were like Grasmere or Glencoe, the sloping fields like Skiddaw. In this brilliant alien world, with the brassy sea all round and the shadows of the shrouds sharply etched on the bellying sails, it was a comfort to think of home.

Between four and five on that Thursday afternoon, the merchant ships in the convoy entered the Bay of Gibraltar and anchored in thirty-six fathoms, half a mile from the landing-place of the Rock. The bay was full of ships—the frigates *Maidstone*, *Medusa* and *Amphion*, sloops and bomb ships, colliers and merchant brigs. It had been an unusually fast passage from Portsmouth, with no really rough weather, the *Speedwell* had never once shipped a wave. In eleven days from its start, half Coleridge's journey was done. He had started using a new notebook that morning, and he wrote in it that he was continuing with his "Memorabilia from Portsmouth, Monday April 9th, 1804, to Gibraltar, and whithersoever else God will or suffer me to go".

XIV·Thursday 19th April

Coleridge did not get ashore that evening, as the quarantine authorities in Gibraltar did not give the *Speedwell* disembarkation clearance till next morning. He spent the evening writing to his friends, to take advantage of this first opportunity of posting letters home. His letter to Southey, though finished, had been kept open so that, by simply underlining the word "Gibraltar", he could indicate rapidly that they had arrived, and then seal and post the letter at once, so as not to lose a chance of an immediate homebound mail; but in fact the letter did not go till four days later, when Coleridge added a postscript, and it did not reach London for another month.

The last part of his letter to Southey was a diatribe against James Tobin, who had seen Coleridge off when he left London. Coleridge had been explaining in his letter to Southey that he had drunk nothing but lemonade on his voyage so far, and he added "so very little does any thing grow into a Habit with me". This reminded him of Tobin, who had gone on cramming officious and unwelcome advice against bad habits into Coleridge's ear right up to the moment when he stepped into the coach for Portsmouth. Tobin had a "rage of *advising*, and of *discussing characters*", and since he also had a "marvellous Genius at utterly misunderstanding what he hears, transposing words often in a manner that would be ludicrous if one did not suspect that his Blindness had a share in producing it", he was "a sad Mischief-maker, and with the best intentions a manufacturer and propagator of calumnies".

James Webbe Tobin, son of a planter in the West Indian island of Nevis, was educated at Bristol Grammar School and at Oxford, and was intended for the Church, but was debarred from this by his loss of sight. For the last eight years he had been living in London, in gloomy chambers in Barnard's Inn, with his brother John who was a solicitor, but whose real interest was the drama. John Tobin wrote one unsuccessful play after another, and eventually died of tuberculosis just before one of his plays was at last performed in a London theatre. The brothers knew most members of Coleridge's circle—Wordsworth (who addressed James in one of his poems as "dear Brother Jem"), Tom Wedgwood, Lamb and Humphry Davy, who had a young relation of James's as his assistant when he was in charge of the Pneumatic Institution in Bristol. Coleridge included James Tobin in one of his imaginary colonies of intellectuals, with Wordsworth, Southey and Davy, but he was fonder of John Tobin, a more relaxed and congenial character, and was suspicious of James's propensity to gossip and interference, though this did not stop him from making indiscreet confidences to James. The blind brother could not stop lecturing everyone within reach, above all his easy-going brother, who was perpetually being reproved for his carelessness and improvidence. Altercations raged at Barnard's Inn, though nothing could really penetrate John's good-natured calm, and the brothers remained devoted to each other.

Coleridge had no such armour against officious advice as John Tobin had. James's parting lecture had hurt and infuriated him; he brooded over it during the voyage to Gibraltar, and planned a forceful letter to James about it, and on this evening in Gibraltar Bay he actually wrote it. "Men who habitually enjoy robust Health, have too generally the trick, and a very cruel one it is, of imagining that they discover the secret of all their Acquaintances' Ill health in some Malpractice or other" he began, and went on to point out that this deprived genuine sufferers of much-needed sympathy, and alarmed their family and friends. He accused Tobin of presumption in giving uncalled-for advice and passing judgements, and of gossip and mischief-making under the excuse of sincerity. He slightly softened the end of this trenchant letter by praising Tobin's integrity and concern for his friends' welfare. But advice-giving was always a mistake; Poole's advice, for instance, had had many ill effects, while Wordsworth's consistent abstention from advice had done nothing but good.

James Tobin was naturally not much delighted by this letter; he drily acknowledged Coleridge's "letter of advice against advising, and other censorious matters". Coleridge had made an enemy, able to do him considerable harm, as he was later to discover. But he had always resented being given advice, and disliked those who gave it; Wordsworth's reserve and non-interference suited him perfectly, though it did him a disservice in the end. Years later, through the treachery of a third person, Wordsworth's contemptuous opinion of Coleridge's opium addiction reached Coleridge's ears, exaggerated and distorted in the telling, and hurt him cruelly. Wordsworth might have been a better friend if he had spoken out earlier. Perhaps it would have made no difference. Coleridge was weak-willed but not easily swayed; the oscillations came from within—outside pressure did not much move him.

Certainly pressure from James Tobin was not likely to do so. Different theories of what Tobin's advice was about have been suggested: that it was against the habit of getting into debt, that it was about Coleridge's relations with James Mackintosh. A debt of Coleridge's to Tobin himself was certainly mentioned in Tobin's parting lecture, and—as will be seen—Tobin later created a fine imbroglio between Coleridge and the Mackintosh faction. But the main warning was against Coleridge's opium habit, and general intemperance; Coleridge's letters to Tobin and Southey make that clear. He told Southey that he had drunk nothing but lemonade during the voyage so far, and that this proved that he was not a slave to alcohol or any other habit; and this reminded him of Tobin's criticism of his "malpractice", typical of an unimaginative healthy man who did not believe in the reality of other and less fortunate men's illnesses, but attributed them to some avoidable habit. At this date Coleridge had not yet quite admitted even to himself, much less to others, that he was addicted to opium; he still maintained that it was a necessary occasional medicine for someone with his poor health.

During his stay in London before leaving for Malta, Coleridge had delivered himself into Tobin's hands. He had called on the lawyer and philosopher Sir James Mackintosh, chiefly out of courtesy and at the request of his friends Thomas Poole and Tom Wedgwood. Mackintosh had married Catherine Allen, one of three sisters, the other two of whom were married to two of Tom Wedgwood's brothers, Josiah and John. Josiah and Tom Wedgwood between them provided Coleridge's only secure income, an annuity of £150.

Coleridge had a poor opinion of Mackintosh, partly because of his attacks on Godwin. Mackintosh had talents but no genius, in Coleridge's opinion, he was entertaining but superficial and cold-hearted. In moments of exasperation Coleridge had described him as "the great Dung-fly" and had written opprobrious verses about his waxy face, black teeth and blacker heart. Fluent and learned as he was, he had no originality; he ought to have "Warehouse to let!" written on his forehead.

However Coleridge agreed to call on Mackintosh in London. He expected—or later said that he had expected—that Mackintosh would simply talk to him about his metaphysical writings. But Mackintosh, who had recently been knighted and was just about to leave for India to take up the appointment of Recorder of Bombay, was loftily condescending to Coleridge, offering to get him a job as his subordinate in Bombay. Coleridge was not pleased, and poured out his feelings to Tobin, whom he met the same day at Humphry Davy's, and to Poole, to whom he wrote that Mackintosh "assured me *on his Honor—on his Soul!!!* (N.B. *His* Honor!!) (N.B. *his* Soul!!) that he was sincere.—Lilibullero—whoo! whoo! whoo!—Good morning, Sir James".

If Coleridge said to Tobin what he wrote to Poole, Tobin had plenty of material for tale-bearing; and he did bear the tale. When Coleridge got back from Malta in 1806 he found that the Wedgwood family were decidedly cool towards him, mainly as a result of Tobin's report of what he had said about Mackintosh. Coleridge wrote to Josiah Wedgwood to refute Tobin's report, to maintain that he had simply mentioned Mackintosh's kindness "quietly and respectfully" to Tobin that day at Davy's, and to point out that Tobin, though a worthy man, was a very mischievous one, and reported what he expected to hear, and imagined he had heard, not what he actually heard.

Coleridge's efforts were in vain, the damage was done. Josiah Wedgwood had other causes of dissatisfaction with him, but his incautious words about Josiah's brother-in-law, resented still more by the Wedgwood sisters who anyway disliked Coleridge, hardened Josiah's heart against his protégé, and in 1812 he withdrew his half of the annuity to Coleridge, though he never explained why. "I had ample reason for what I did" was all he would say.

Coleridge never paid enough attention to the relationships between other people to enable him to realize that they might compare notes about him and what he had said to them; the embarrassments and coolnesses which resulted when they did so, always came as a shock to him. He would say one thing to one correspondent, and another to another, as though there were no such thing in the world as a tale-bearer, and then be astonished and wounded when, his letters having been passed round, he was reproached for speaking ill of friends and benefactors. Apart from the generous and peace-making Lamb, who never passed on comments likely to give pain, most of Coleridge's correspondents— even such thorough well-wishers as Lady Beaumont—showed his letters just where they could do most harm. Like all of us, Coleridge adapted his personality to his correspondent; if he was flippant to Lamb and sanctimonious to Estlin about the same incident, it was partly because he knew that Lamb had a sense of humour and Estlin had not. But he was incautious beyond the limits of such normal variations of tone. He could analyse his own character so finely, admit his more sympathetic faults so candidly, that it seemed to him that everyone must recognize and accept the authenticity of the particular Coleridge self-portrait presented to them, and be unable to conjure up any other which might conflict with it.

XV · *Thursday 19th April*

Coleridge in his turn could have told tales of Tobin if he had wanted to. "I used to be much amused with Tobin and Godwin" he wrote many years later about his London stay in 1804. "Tobin would pester me with stories of Godwin's dulness; and upon his departure Godwin would drop in just to say that Tobin was more dull than ever".

Coleridge saw a lot of Godwin during his time in London, a good deal more than he wanted to, in fact, as Godwin would haunt him, in his busiest moments, with a five-act tragedy, full of flatnesses and incongruities, on which he wanted Coleridge's opinion. Coleridge knew that the play was hopelessly bad—"it will die the Death of a Red hot Poker in water, all one Hiss"—and he grudged the hours he had to spend on going through the manuscript when he had not got enough time for his own most urgent concerns; but, as he said, "what can a decently good-natured man say to a Brother Bard who tells you that it is of importance to his Happiness and Pecuniary Circumstances?"

Coleridge had known William Godwin for ten years, and had at times been very friendly with him, though in the last three years they had seen less of each other and their correspondence had flagged. Even Godwin's colossal vanity recognized the power of Coleridge's genius; he actually admitted that his own mind was "indebted for improvement" to Coleridge's, and he often consulted Coleridge about his hopes of succeeding as a dramatist. Coleridge had begun by admiring Godwin for his courage in writing *Political Justice*, and had even written a sonnet to him; then when he had read more of Godwin's works, he had a reaction against him; finally, when his own mind matured and became calmer and more tolerant, and when he actually met Godwin in the flesh, they became friends, specially as Coleridge was disgusted by the desertion and ingratitude of Godwin's former disciples.

When one reads Godwin's letters of the early 1800's, one wonders how anyone of any sensibility could have tolerated him. The personality revealed in his letters is extraordinarily dislikable— smug, self-righteous, self-pitying, hypocritical, an offence-taker and a grudge-bearer, a sanctimonious and shameless borrower, a quarreller whose life was punctuated with broken-off friendships. He described himself as "extremely modest", but had no hesitation in pronouncing that he was widely loved and respected and one of the best-known men of his age. In some ways he understood and analysed his own prickly temperament fairly well, but he had no idea—far less than even Coleridge had—of the impression that he made on other men; he thought they all saw him as he saw himself— a reserved, high-minded, irresistibly attractive giant.

On 14th April, when Coleridge's convoy was in the Bay of Biscay, Godwin wrote a begging letter to Tom Wedgwood, asking for £100.

"It is with the utmost reluctance of feeling that I obtrude on you the following statement. I know not whether I am entitled to the possession of several opulent friends: this has been almost universally the lot of persons of as much literary publicity as myself: it has been my fortune never, except you, to have had one". He went on to say that he had been working to make money by writing plays, had borrowed £100 from an unspecified young man to keep his family while he was writing a play, but it had been unsuccessful and he had never been able to repay the £100, which the young man now wanted back. He emphasized how hard he and his wife worked to support a numerous family. Would Tom Wedgwood advance the £100? He then belatedly remembered that Wedgwood, to whom he had obviously not given a thought for years, till he needed money from him, was supposed to be an invalid, so he slid in an enquiry about his health. "Though it is now a very long time since I have heard from, or seen you, yet I have occasionally the satisfaction, I wish I could say the pleasure, of hearing concerning you from Tobin, Coleridge and others. The last opportunity of this sort was a letter by you to Coleridge, a short time before his departure, in which you spoke of your health as being a little better than it had been some time before. What pleasure would it afford to me, and to everyone that knows you, could we have a well-grounded prospect of its being ultimately restored. With sincere affection, W. Godwin".

The most extraordinary part of this revolting letter is its assumption that authors are *entitled* to have rich friends, and that Godwin had somehow been defrauded by having only one. It is true that the age of literary patronage was only recently over, but such a claim comes very oddly from someone of Godwin's political and economic opinions. He got his £100, however. Tom Wedgwood, ill and wretched as he was that spring, hopeless of recovery and longing for death, answered by return, sending the money, with a roughly honest but mainly kind letter. He gave short shrift to Godwin's theory about his right to have rich friends. "I have no opinion of the good, upon the whole, resulting from great facility in the opulent, in yielding to requests of the needy". Every man should expect the possibility of financial distress, which should quicken his ability to provide for himself; half the industry of the country would be destroyed were the idea to prevail that "the rich held funds for the needy", though real suffering should be relieved, and avarice was detestable. He ended by saying that he admired Godwin's struggles and moral feelings, though not necessarily his politics and philosophy.

The feelings about Godwin of most of his contemporaries in the early 1800s were warmed by their admiration of the man he had been—the courageous political philosopher, vilified for and endangered by his beliefs, the inspirer of the young, the generous supporter of his spendthrift siblings, the husband of whom Mary Wollstonecraft had said on her deathbed "He is the kindest, best man in the world". But now he was married to a very different and infinitely inferior woman, a bad-tempered malicious domineering scold who did her best to alienate him from his friends. It was she who was responsible for the worst part of the "dreadful Rumpus", as Coleridge called it, which took place this spring between him and Godwin.

The two men dined with Charles and Mary Lamb on 2nd February. The conversation turned on magazines and reviews, and how bad they mostly were, and Coleridge revealed that he and Southey had often talked of doing a review page in an evening paper; it had been a favourite plan with him for two years.

"A plan which no man who had a spark of honest pride could join with, no man not the slave of the grossest Egotism, could write in" was Godwin's comment.

"Don't you and others already do what I'm proposing, in Prefaces?" retorted Coleridge.

"Aye—in *prefaces*—that is quite a different thing".

Coleridge angrily pointed out the rudeness of Godwin's comment, specially as the scheme had the approval of Wordsworth and Southey as well as himself.

"Yes Sir! just so! of Mr Southey" answered Godwin, and launched into a diatribe against Southey in terms which would have been much more appropriate to himself. Coleridge made fun of

Godwin's notion that what would be gross egotism in an evening paper was manly discriminating self-respect in a preface, and, becoming angrier and more sarcastic, suggested that Godwin should show more reverence to men who were his betters.

After a time the argument died down, and Godwin left the party for a while. Coleridge meant to leave too, but Godwin had begged him to wait till his return. Mary Lamb mixed Coleridge a glass of punch which was a good deal stronger than he realized. While he was drinking it, in came Mrs Godwin and some other guests, and presently Godwin returned and they all sat down to supper. Coleridge was by now tired of the company of "this dim-headed Prig of a Philosophicide", and also rather drunk; he talked and laughed at supper, but was sick at heart, and when Godwin insisted on reopening the argument, at first begged him not to. But Godwin had been egged on by his wife, who had twitted him at having been defeated by Coleridge, as though he couldn't call his soul his own; and although—or possibly because—Godwin realized that Coleridge was tipsy, he dragged up the argument again, and finally evoked a furious harangue in which Coleridge drew some very unflattering comparisons between him and Southey, Wordsworth and himself, as men, as writers, and as benefactors of society, and attacked Godwin's atheism. It was one of Coleridge's most sensational performances, a flood of scornful and ferocious eloquence, which lasted an hour and a half, and annihilated Godwin.

As Coleridge walked home that evening, he was still convinced that he had been in the right but, not knowing of Mrs Godwin's mischief-making, he felt sorry he had attacked her husband in her presence. Next morning he woke up deeply ashamed at having taken part in such a disgraceful scene, and wrote to Godwin to apologize to him and his wife, though he still felt that Godwin had provoked him by attacking Southey. He sent accounts of the "direful Quarrel" to his wife, to the Wordsworths and to Southey, regretting that he had been so violent and so drunk, and saying there had been a reconciliation next day, though he was still scornful about Godwin's intellectual blindness; "the fool's conduct richly merited a flogging, but not with a scourge of Scorpions". It was not till three days later, when he called on the Lambs to apologize for making such a scene in their house, that he heard the full story of the part played by Mrs Godwin in envenoming the argument, after which he lost all feelings of remorse towards either of the Godwins, and told Southey that he was resolved to be more careful in future about making friends with men essentially uncongenial to him.

XVI · *Thursday 19th April*

Southey seized on Coleridge's admission that he ought to choose his friends with more care. It enabled Southey to say what he had long felt needed saying to Coleridge, and his reply is an important statement of the concern felt by Coleridge's more cautious friends about the situations into which his impulsive advances led him. "I am not sorry you gave Godwin a dressing, and should not be sorry if he were occasionally to remember it with the comfortable reflection 'in vino veritas'; for, in plain truth, already it does vex me to see you so lavish of the outward and visible signs of friendship, and to know that a set of fellows whom you do not care for and ought not to care for, boast everywhere of your intimacy, and with good reason, to the best of their understanding. You have accustomed yourself to talk affectionately, and write affectionately, to your friends, till the expressions of affection flow by habit in your conversation, and in your letters, and pass for more than they are worth; the worst of all this is, that your letters will one day rise up in judgement against you (for be sure, that hundreds which you have forgotten, are hoarded up for some Curl or Phillips of the next generation), and you will be convicted of a double dealing which, though you do not design, you certainly do practise. And now that I *am* writing affectionately *more meo*, I will let out a little more. You say in yours to Sara, that you love and honour me; upon my soul I believe you: but if I did not thoroughly believe it before, your saying so is the thing of all things that would make me open my eyes and look about me to see if I were not deceived: perhaps I am too intolerant to these kind of phrases; but, indeed, when they are true, they may be excused, and when they are not, there is no excuse for them . . . There is a something outlandish in saying them, more akin to a French embrace than an English shake by the hand, and I would have you leave off saying them to those whom you actually do love, that if this should not break off the habit of applying them to indifferent persons, the disuse may at least make a difference. Your feelings go naked, I cover mine with a bear-skin; I will not say that you harden yours by your mode, but I am sure that mine are the warmer for their clothing . . . It is possible, or probable, that I err as much as you in an opposite extreme, and may make enemies where you would make friends; but there is a danger that you may sometimes excite dislike in persons of whose approbation you would yourself be desirous. You know me well enough to know in what temper this has been written, and to know that it has been some exertion; for the same habit which makes me prefer sitting silent to offering contradiction, makes me often withhold censure when perhaps, in strictness of moral duty, it ought to be applied. The medicine might have been sweetened perhaps; but, dear Coleridge, take the simple bitters, and leave the sweetmeats by themselves.

"That ugly-nosed Godwin has led me to this. I daresay he deserved all you gave him. . . . If he had not married again, I would still have some bowels of compassion for him, but to take another wife with the picture of Mary Wollstonecraft in his house! Augh!"

Coleridge, who did not like advice, would not relish such a letter as this, and when he told Southey two months later how much he resented Tobin's advice, no doubt there was an implication that Southey's own offering had not been welcome. But he would have done well to heed this letter, which superficially may sound priggish but really shows a manly and thoughtful concern for Coleridge's true welfare. It was curiously echoed four years later by Wordsworth, in his drier style, when he told Coleridge "You precipitate yourself into friendships (amities if you think the word too strong) and trust to Providence for pulling you out of them . . . I am not fond of making myself hastily beloved and admired, you take more delight in it than a wise man ought".

"Your letters will one day rise up in judgement against you"; Southey's warning was terribly prescient. One after another of Coleridge's biographers, faced by these embarrassing self-contradictory posturing documents, have found their admiration for Coleridge turning into exasperation and even contempt. Some of them write about him as though he were Frederick Rolfe, and every accusation that Coleridge too was shifty, ungrateful, unreliable, that he exploited his attractiveness to get money and hospitality out of his benefactors, and then turned and rent them afterwards, that he thought the world owed him love and a living but that he need not give anything in return—all this can be supported by evidence from his own letters. "It is no new thing for people to take sudden and hot Likings to me" he told his wife complacently, and it was true— when they were actually with him they were all enthralled by his eloquence and charm, and he saw that this was so. What he did not see was their reaction afterwards, when he was no longer present, the disappointment that even good friends like Humphry Davy some- times felt. He judged their feelings for him only by their enthralment in his presence, and then was appalled, and felt himself betrayed, when some accident revealed that their enthralment was not the whole of their feeling for him. Then he would turn nasty, and write savage jokes about good friends like Poole, and even Lamb. A kind of coarsening is apparent in his letters of early 1804, a spitefulness about other writers such as Rogers and Campbell who had never done him any harm, a lack of truth, a hollowness of protestation, which forebodes what he confessed ten years later, that the "dirty business of laudanum" had made him a liar and a trickster.

Though this side of Coleridge was only one aspect of a many-faceted character, it was the side that strong-willed men of talent but no genius, in his own age and in ours, saw first and most. Southey saw it; so did Poole, who while acknowledging Coleridge's splendid abilities, added that he "feels the justice of Providence in the want of those inferior abilities which are necessary to the rational discharge of the common duties of life". So did Mackintosh, who thought that

Coleridge's want of application made all his conversation muddled and unclear, and Farington, who saw little but confusion and vanity in Coleridge's performance as a talker, when he got home after an evening of unwillingly spellbound listening and tried to sum up in his diary what he had heard.

One new acquaintance made by Coleridge during his stay in London was perfectly representative of this type of reaction to his personality. John Rickman, a friend of Lamb and Southey, was at this time Secretary to the Speaker of the House of Commons. He lived in an official house opposite the east side of Westminster Hall, reached through an archway and a small courtyard, all long since vanished. He had a charming garden with a lawn surrounded by cherry trees and gooseberry bushes and a hedge of jasmine, and he entertained many literary friends, Coleridge among them, to four o'clock dinners in his book room. Rickman was shrewd, honest, well-informed and hard-working, but censorious, irascible, and quite unsympathetic with any kind of weakness. He was hospitable to Coleridge, and advised him about his passage to Malta, though he was not pleased when Coleridge's correspondence was sent under cover to him to avoid the payment of postage. Coleridge wrote him an effusive letter before he left London, expressing admiration of Rickman's character and self-control, and confidence that they would have become friends if time had allowed. He was aware, he told Southey, that Rickman, "that STERLING Man", did not altogether like him, but he would have been miserable had he known what Rickman wrote to Southey about him on the eve of his departure. "I have just heard from Coleridge, that he goes for Portsmouth tomorrow evening. He is very unwell in body and his mind very depressed, and very excitable by objects to other men scarce visible or feelable. Your prudence will not tell this to his fireside, and the voyage may cure him. If he dies, it will be from a sulky imagination, produced from the general cause of such things, i.e. want of regular work or application: which is a great pity". Four days later he wrote again. "I am a little annoyed by a habit of *assentation*, which I fancy I perceive in him; and cannot but think that he likes to talk well, rather than to give or receive much information. I understand he is terribly pestered with invitations to go to parties, as a singer does, to amuse the guests by his talent; a hateful task I should think: I would rather not talk finely, than talk to such a purpose".

Thus they all—Rickman, Southey, even Wordsworth—measured themselves against Coleridge, and decided that they were taller men —morally taller, at least, with a more manly reserve and decorum. Men like these, and still more men like Tobin, could not give Coleridge the help he most needed. Brooding about Tobin's officiousness while the *Speedwell* drove southwards towards Gibraltar, Coleridge had written in his notebook: "Of your *good* man, who can conceive no object of goodness not starving or dying. These men drive a *Trade*: and every Thing smells of the Shop". Men who reserved their compassion for the Deserving Poor could not help Coleridge. It was the simple admirers, with no pretensions to intellectual equality, like John Morgan and James Gillman, and those few who combined real genius with humility—men like Charles Lamb and Humphry Davy—who could accept and love Coleridge as he was. Even Lamb was once briefly estranged, when, as so often happened to Coleridge, something he had said about Lamb to a person supposed trustworthy was reported with additions and distortions to Lamb himself. Then Lamb wrote him that letter which is the most terrible of all indictments of Coleridge, because it was made by a man with no envy or meanness in his heart. Under the witty guise of a set of theological propositions, Lamb asked Coleridge whether he was not a lying angel, a sneering seraph, whether he was capable of love, whether he did not live in an eternity of complacent self-satisfaction, whether he was not damned without knowing it?

Lamb found that he had been misled, the estrangement ended, and they were friends for all the rest of their lives, a friendship beside which the disapproval of men like Rickman and Farington was insignificant. But it was Humphry Davy who, at the moment of Coleridge's departure into exile, gave him the perfect reassurance that he was loved and valued by those whose good opinion was worth having, specially by the young, to whom he opened new worlds of thought and hope.

In 1804 Davy was still only twenty-five, but already a well-known man. Coleridge had known him since, as a twenty-year-old, he had been appointed to the Pneumatic Institution in Bristol. He was a friend of Southey and Tobin, too, and when he came to London in 1801 to take up a post as Director of the Laboratory at the Royal Institution, he met all Coleridge's London circle and made a great many friends of his own. This curly-haired young Cornishman, whose harsh but carefully modulated voice could explain scientific facts so lucidly, was in constant request as a diner-out, and his lectures at the Royal Institution were always crowded. By 1802 he had become Professor of Chemistry to the Institution, and he lived in rooms there, piled with books and papers but plainly furnished and with no ornaments except a little porcelain Venus given to him by Tom Wedgwood. Here by himself he ate an austere meal of fish on the days when he was concocting his carefully prepared and rehearsed and brilliantly successful lectures; and here he entertained Coleridge and other friends to dinner on less occupied afternoons. Davy was a poet as well as a scientific genius, and his candid and ardent mind appealed to the best side of Coleridge's nature. Just as Coleridge was leaving London for Portsmouth, Davy sent him a farewell letter to say how much he owed to him, and what great hopes he had for him. Coleridge's conversation had elevated Davy's feelings and enlarged his ideas, and however far away he went, he would live on in Davy's mind as a "*recollection* possessed of creative energy, as an Imagination winged with fire inspiriting and rejoicing". Coleridge must give to the world proofs of that power which those who already knew him admired in him; perhaps in his exile he would find that freedom from distraction which would enable him to fulfil his destiny as the historian of the philosophy of feeling. Davy ended his heartening letter (which, unlike the unwanted advice of the officious, evoked from Coleridge a reply not only grateful, but humble and sincere much beyond his wont) by a heroic invocation: "Do not in any way dissipate your noble nature, do not give up your birthright. May you soon recover perfect health; the health of strength and happiness! May you soon return to us confirmed in all the powers essential to the exertion of genius—You were born for your Country and your native land must be the scene of your activity. I shall expect the time when your spirit bursting through the clouds of ill health will appear to *all men* not as an uncertain and brilliant *flame* but as a fair and permanent *light*, fixed though constantly in motion, as a sun which gives its fire not only to its attendant *Planets*; but which sends *beams* from all its parts into all worlds. My blessings attend you, my dear friend! Do not forget me: we live for different ends, and with different habits and pursuits; but our feelings with regard to each other have, I believe, never altered. They must continue; they can have no natural death; and, I trust, they can never be destroyed by fortune, chance or accident".

XVII · *Friday 20th April*

Coleridge went ashore in Gibraltar on Friday morning, when the *Speedwell* had been given her quarantine clearance. Walking along the sea rampart and then up through the town, he was fascinated by the lively spectacle of the crowds jostling through the hot stinking streets and strolling under the poplars in the central parade. He struck off a set of vivid pen-portraits of the figures he saw: a muleteer with grinning teeth like a monkey's, wearing a black velvet cap and with his stick thrust through the back of his waistband; boys collecting refuse and orange peel into the panniers of their meagre donkeys; porters, six abreast, stopping to rest and blocking the way; Jews with fine high-bred faces and black bombazine robes like college gowns; a goat with its forefeet in the panniers of a horse, from which it was stealing hay; groups of dirty Spaniards with their cloaks falling in elegant folds; runaway sailors, pretty dowdy Greek women with huge ear-rings; English officers and their wives. He felt that his words were inadequate to describe such a scene; what was wanted was a young painter with a turn for depicting characters—such a man could spend a year on the Rock with advantage, there was enough material for a dozen plates by Hogarth.

Coleridge delivered letters of introduction to a gunner major, Ralph Adye, and to the garrison chaplain Mr Frome, and then explored the Rock. He followed the winding road up to Europa Point, enjoying the sight of sheets of pink geranium hanging over the walls, and prickly pears, and a broom bush, in full flower and the size of a tree, with a young donkey no bigger than a mastiff tethered under it. Masses of wild flowers grew among the grey rocks, some of them old acquaintances from England which Coleridge recognized, others new to him.

He wandered slowly on, full of calm enjoyment and happy recollections, till it was time to return to Griffiths Hotel to dine with Captain Findlay of the *Speedwell* and a party of seventeen other masters of merchant ships. The food at dinner was indifferent and the wine fiery, and it was a noisy party, with a lot of disputing about facts, on the lines of "I had it from a man on the Spot, who *saw* it"; Coleridge said to himself that he had never been with four or five "Men on the Spot" without their contradicting each other about what they actually saw. But he did exchange a lot of very interesting news about the war at sea.

He learned that the West India convoy which had sailed from Portsmouth five days before his own, had come to grief. The frigate *Apollo*, Captain Dixon, and forty of the convoy had been wrecked near Cape Mondego on the coast of Portugal, and Captain Dixon and many of his officers and crew were drowned. Some said that the disaster was due to stormy weather, others that there was an error in Captain Dixon's compasses. When Coleridge was waiting at Portsmouth for his own convoy to sail, he had felt envious at the sight of the West India convoy setting off. Now he congratulated himself on his comparative good fortune, and then felt rather ashamed of such a feeling, and tried to work out the rights of it. "It is impossible not to *feel* events like these, as something *providential*: tho' the Reason denounces the notion as *superstitious*, and indeed arrogant (for who are we, that we should be *favourites* with Heaven to the exclusion of the W. India Ships?) yet the feeling remains—neither greater nor less—common to all men, whatever their opinions may be, and amid all differences of knowledge and understanding. It must therefore be right at the bottom; and probably needs only a wiser interpretation to appear so".

The loss of the West India convoy was not the only naval disaster about which Coleridge heard at Gibraltar. Even before he went ashore he had seen a newspaper report from Barcelona with news of two further losses, both severe blows to the Mediterranean Fleet; and the party at Griffiths Hotel, and others within earshot, were deeply concerned with this news. Eighteen days earlier, on 2nd April, the store-ship *Hindostan*, bound for Malta, had caught fire in the Bay of Rosas and been totally destroyed. The *Hindostan* had a valuable cargo of stores of all kinds which were desperately needed by the Mediterranean Fleet. Coleridge's announcement of her destruction to the party at Griffiths was overheard by a naval officer who had himself travelled in the *Hindostan* from England as far as Gibraltar, and was thunderstruck to hear of her loss. He told Coleridge that she carried a hundred artificers in addition to her crew, and that her cargo was valued at £300,000, and was considered so vital that though she carried more than forty guns of her own, she was given a frigate to escort her to Malta. Another man, who had recently arrived from Malta, joined in to say that the ships there were desperately in need of the stores carried by the *Hindostan*.

Nelson, when he heard of the loss of the ship, and that nothing had been saved—"not even a second shirt for anyone"—owned it was a grievous blow, but with care and attention by every captain in the Fleet, they would get through the summer somehow without the expected stores. He thought the fire probably started from a breakage of the medicine chests, whose contents were highly inflammable, or from sea-water getting into the hold so that the stores got wet and started to heat up. The great thing was that, by the "cool and collected conduct" of the Captain, and the extraordinary exertions of all concerned, all but four of the ship's company were saved. Captain Le Gros was afterwards court-martialled, but honourably acquitted.

This was not the end of the tale of disasters. When the *Hindostan* caught fire, H.M.S. *Juno*, which was cruising off the Spanish coast to protect British shipping, left her station to go to the aid of the *Hindostan*. As a result, the cutter *Swift*, on her way to Nelson with despatches from the Admiralty, was captured by a French privateer. The *Swift* had only eight four-pounder guns and twenty-three men; the French privateer *L'Esperance* had ten guns and fifty-four men, so the *Swift* had little chance, specially as her commander, Lieutenant Leake, was killed at the very beginning of the engagement. There was a report that all the despatches had been thrown overboard before the cutter was captured, but this was doubtful.

Nelson, who was cruising off Toulon in the *Victory*, had heard of this catalogue of catastrophes the day before Coleridge and his party thrashed them out in the noisy hotel in Gibraltar. Nelson was deeply concerned at the loss of the *Hindostan*, but the capture of the *Swift* made him really angry. How could the Admiralty have been so utterly imprudent as to send unciphered despatches in a ship of that size? "Every Jack in Diplomatic affairs is intrusted with a cipher, but an Admiral Commander in Chief not". He was convinced that all the despatches had been captured intact and sent straight to Napoleon; "I wish they were in his throat" Nelson added. He could only hope that the Foreign Office and other Government departments, unlike the Admiralty, had been too wise to entrust unciphered despatches to such a little ship. What would the governments of Russia, Sardinia, Naples, Turkey, Egypt, think if they heard that their affairs and plans had been discussed in despatches which had fallen into the hands of the French? "The loss of the Hindostan, was great enough; but, for importance, it is lost in comparison with the probable knowledge the Enemy will obtain of our connexions with Foreign Countries! Foreigners for ever say, and it is true—'We dare not trust England; one way or another, we are sure to be committed!' "

Nelson's rage was aggravated by the fear that Napoleon was now reading not only Admiralty and Foreign Office secret despatches, but also Emma Hamilton's letters which had been sent by the *Swift*. As Nelson sat in his black leather armchair in his day cabin in the

Friday 20th April

Victory, dictating to his secretary Dr Scott his vehement letters to Admiral St Vincent, Lord Hobart and Captain Richardson about the capture of the *Swift*, he was also thinking what he would write in his own hand to Emma, later that day. The horizon pivoted across the nine sash windows in the stern of the cabin as the *Victory* rolled in the perpetual swell of the Gulf of Lions, and the black and white checks on the canvas carpet heaved and glared. In mid-afternoon the band struck up on deck, and Nelson sat down to dinner with his staff in his spacious dining cabin, opening onto the day cabin. Nelson's men probably did not grudge him his three big cabins—they did not grudge him anything—but when one visits the *Victory* today, and sees the dark oppressively low quarters where 850 men ate at rude tables between the guns and slept in hammocks, and then the suite of many-windowed airy cabins, thirty-five feet wide at their widest, furnished with handsome mahogany chairs, tables and desks, and hung with pictures and embroidered bed-curtains, which were Nelson's quarters, one does wonder how much the contrast was noted then. The difference was equally striking in the meals provided; at Nelson's dinner table three courses and a dessert were always served, with champagne and claret, though he himself often ate no more than a small plate of macaroni and a chicken wing, with one glass of champagne, and some watered wine afterwards.

His letter to Emma contained some pleasant news, about the presents of Cyprus wine and sweet-smelling Spanish honey that he was sending home to her, but it was mostly about his mortification at the loss of her letters to him in the *Swift*. "As I do not know what letters of yours are in her, I cannot guess what will be said. I suppose, there will be a publication". He feared that in any case all their letters to each other were read en route, so he warned her never to sign her name, and that his own letters would never give anything away except "eternal attachment and affection for you; and that I care not who knows". All the same, he sent Dr Scott to Barcelona to try and recover Lady Hamilton's letters from the French Consul there, who had keenly read them all—they would probably be published in a book by the French authorities, "but from us, what can they find out? That I love you most dearly, and hate the French most damnably". A picture of Lady Hamilton had been sent in the *Swift* with her letters, and had also fallen into the hands of the French Consul in Barcelona, who was said to admire it so much that he had kept it for himself instead of sending it on to Napoleon who—Nelson was persuaded—would also have been captivated by it.

Nelson also wrote on 19th April to his niece Charlotte, daughter of his parson brother, who was staying with Lady Hamilton and had got a good report for loving Horatia. "What hearts those must have, who do not!" wrote Horatia's doting father to her far from doting mother. "But, thank God, she shall not be dependent on any of them" added Nelson, who little knew what was in store for his only child. His letter to his niece is an extraordinary and painful piece of anxious equivocation. He referred to Horatia as a "dear little orphan" whose parents were lost, but who had money of her own. "I shall cherish her to the last moment of my life, and *curse* them who *curse* her, and Heaven *bless* them who *bless* her! Dear innocent! she can have injured no one. I am glad to hear that she is attached to you; and, if she takes after her parents, so she will to those who are kind to her". What can Charlotte Nelson have made of her uncle's passionate devotion to Horatia? Did she know or suspect who the "little orphan's lost parents" really were?

Though Nelson was anxious and angry about the effects of the *Swift*'s capture, he was confident about the general situation. He was in constant expectation of the emergence of the French Fleet from Toulon, and of the battle which would follow. He was sure it would be a glorious one; not sure he would survive it; but determined to act so that "my friends shall not blush for me", and confident that the whole Fleet would behave gallantly. He had recently received a letter from Lord Hobart conveying the King's approbation of his achievements (four days later he was to be promoted Vice-Admiral of the White, though he did not hear of this for another three months), and in his reply he said "My eye is constantly fixed upon Toulon, and I have no great reason to believe that the French will escape me whatever may be their destination: and then it is with real pleasure that I can state to your Lordship, and request you will state it to the King, that no Fleet was ever in higher discipline, and health, and good humour, than the one I have the honour to command; and whenever we fall in with the Enemy's Fleet, (if I do my duty), the happiest result will, I may venture to say, accrue".

XVIII· *Friday 20th April to Tuesday 24th April*

Captain Findlay got very drunk at the party at Griffiths Hotel, and Coleridge had to escort him back to the *Speedwell* and deposit him in his cabin, where the drinking bout continued with three other masters of merchant ships, while Coleridge went to bed, thinking what a mixed day it had been, a mermaid day, half of it sweet tranquillity and tender thoughts, the other half a "scaly obscene Monster-fish" of drunken noise.

Next morning, Saturday, he went ashore again and explored the Rock more thoroughly. He left the road to climb towards the summit of the ridge among pale rocks through patches of wild flowers; the pungent smell of the tansy plants struck upwards as he crushed them under his feet. He reached the Signal House on the seaward peak, where he could see down both sides of the Rock as he sat astraddle the ridge. Southward across the blue and sunny sea were the tumbled pyramids of the mountains behind Ceuta. On the Mediterranean face of the Rock, which plunged nearly fifteen hundred feet to a tiny beach, and among the chaotic rocks and uncouth palmettos which crowned the landward crests of the ridge, there was no sign of human life, and no movement to be seen except an occasional grey streak as one of the Rock apes leapt from one ledge to another. (Plate V). But on the Atlantic side of the Rock there was a vast and moving panorama. Close below him were neat small houses with

V "A perpendicular precipice . . . an unmanageable mass of stone and weeds"; the eastern face of the Rock of Gibraltar from the summit

VI (i) The New Mole of Gibraltar, with Frigates. H.M.S. *Maidstone* was anchored here, to frighten off privateers from the Barbary Coast, before escorting Coleridge's convoy to Malta. *Illustration by J. T. Serres to* The Little Sea Torch, *1801*

(ii) Model of a 32-gun frigate, of H.M.S. *Maidstone*'s class, c. 1805

gardens full of geraniums, shaded by poplars and cypresses and hedged by the weirdly-shaped prickly pears, with leaves like the carved wings of cherubs in some enigmatic temple. Tiny fields of brilliantly green corn, already knee-high, were crammed among the rocks. Down the landward end of the Rock ran the ramparts and towers of the old Moorish fortifications, the rock face was honey-combed with caves within whose openings lurked the grinning mouths of huge guns, the town at the foot of the Rock seethed with life, and the Bay was studded with ships.

Coleridge felt a most unusual well-being. The weather was perfect, a sunshine hot enough to make the shade of the trees feel pleasant and the sea breezes enjoyable. He had shed most of the layers of clothes he had worn when he left England, and was now clad in nankeen trousers and silk stockings, with only one flannel waistcoat. The heat he had experienced in the last few days suited him perfectly, and he was convinced that spending an autumn and winter in such a climate would create him a new man.

A fair breeze had blown him speedily on his way to Gibraltar, a good omen for a man whose imagination so often pictured himself as a ship. He might be destined to spend long years in exile, crossing dangerous seas, seeing strange wonders in the ancient Mediterranean world, living among alien landscapes like the one now spread out below him as he sat perched on the top of the Rock, but he believed in the power of Nature to unify and make sense of all new experience. He thought again, as he had thought two days earlier when he first saw Europe on his left and Africa on his right from the deck of the *Speedwell*, that there was an "inseparable character of Unity" behind the grandeur of these vast landscapes. It was not their strangeness that moved him; distinct and different as they were, they integrated themselves into the country which his imagination already inhabited, among the familiar hills and fields of home, with well-remembered names, where lived all those whom he loved best and who shared his language and beliefs. Sitting there in the quiet heat of noon, he felt his heart kindled by the vision before him, and was content to "know nothing, feel nothing, but the Abiding Things of Nature, great, calm, majestic and one".

H

The power of Nature over his imagination was bound up with his love for Sara Hutchinson. The thought of her was always with him, wherever he was, whatever he was doing—reading, walking, talking about politics, alone and silent on a hilltop or laughing at a dinner-table with a party of drunken sea-captains. Memories of his love, and hopes and dreams of its future, were with him so continually that he felt the thought of Sara as though it were an actual physical pain in his heart, a sore spot on which he could put his finger, something that "wishes and yearns, and stirs and bustles about you, and then stagnates upon you, wishless from excess of wishing". A face in the street could remind him of her, the sweet face of an English officer's wife seen for a moment among the jostling crowds on the Gibraltar quay, but he felt her presence most of all when he was looking at landscapes which recalled the lakes and mountains of Westmorland where he and she had walked. When he tried to visualize her, it was not her face that he saw, but some beautiful place which they had explored together. His mind's eye saw them standing—as perhaps they never had stood in reality, but only in his imagination—by the roaring cascade of Scale Force, so intent that other sightseers by the waterfall had laughed at them for a pair of lovers; or sitting under a rock on a ledge high above Crummock Lake, with Sara kissing his forehead. These dream memories played their contrapuntal harmonies and variations incessantly in his heart, connecting everything that he saw with "one abiding Hope, one Thought, one Love".

He sat musing on the summit of the Rock for a long time. Finally he scrambled down to the road again, pluming himself on an agility almost as good as the apes'. On the way down he found the entrance to St Michael's Cave, and left the dazzling daylight to explore its dim chambers and recesses. He was fascinated by the stalactite shapes, obelisks and thrones and slender trees, and by the mystery of what was literally a cavern measureless to man, for though men had been let down four hundred feet on ropes, with torches in their hands, to the abysses of the cave, they had never reached the bottom. Again he felt the tingle of paramnesia. He had imagined all this long before he saw it. The fourth act of his Spanish tragedy *Osorio*, written in 1797, had depicted just such a cave, an icy trickling darkness where huge chasms opened at one's feet, and torches smoked, and old nightmares stirred in the memory. The Moresco chieftain Isidore in Coleridge's play revealed that he had already seen in a dream the chasm in a cave which he now saw with waking eyes. Now, seven years after that was written, Coleridge himself was near the "Sea Shore on the Coast of Granada" which was the scene of his play, was among Spaniards and Moors (his journal for this day dismisses the Spaniards as "a degraded Race that dishonor Christianity" and the Moors as "wretches that dishonor human Nature"), and was peering down into just such a chasm as he had already seen in an imaginative dream seven years earlier when he was writing his tragedy.

He dined that day with Frome, the garrison chaplain, a pleasant-looking man who gave him the kind of temperate meal that suited him best, and he went back to the *Speedwell* feeling that he had spent the day well and worthily. He congratulated himself on the good effects of a regimen of drinking only beer and lemonade, and on feeling indifferent to wine and actually disliking spirits; brandy and ginger-water, with which he had experimented during the voyage, had been poisonous to his stomach, and mulled wine had made him sick at once, but temperance and the fine weather had made him uncommonly well for the last four days.

Sunday was spent on board the *Speedwell* reading, writing letters and recording the previous day's experience in his notebook. He had started using a new one, black leather with a metal clasp, opening sideways like a book instead of upwards like the previous notebook. Some of its first pages were filled with Coleridge's attempts to draw the outlines of the Rock of Gibraltar, a set of dim hairy scribbles which gave little suggestion of that superb profile. His day of rest was not as propitious as the previous day had been. As he was reading in the *Speedwell*'s cabin, he began to feel suffocated, with cramps in his stomach and legs. Mrs Ireland, the fat passenger, who was also in the cabin, remarked on his stertorous breathing; this broke through Coleridge's absorption with his book, and he looked out of the porthole to see that rain was pouring down. He went up on deck to get some air and found that the wind was in the east, the sky black with clouds, the mountains darkened with rain. The storm blew over, Coleridge felt better and ate a good dinner, but the return of the east wind gave him a bad night, and he was in poor condition, with no appetite, a furred tongue, a fast pulse, and fever smells in his nostrils, when he got up next morning.

Ill as he felt, he went ashore on Monday and called on Major Adye, a former pupil of Coleridge's schoolmaster brother George, who arranged for him to see round the gun batteries, and gave him dinner. Coleridge was feeling rather better by the time he got back to the *Speedwell*, and the night was fine and clear, so he stayed late on deck watching the night sky. The moon was full and had a halo, with a few bright stars at its edge. Flakes of cloud floated across under the moon from the summit of the Rock towards the Spanish mountains. A path of reflected moonlight ran from the shore to within a stone's-throw of the ship, with a dance of insects swarming in it. In the shadow of the ship's mast and rigging, the moon path was broken up into rapidly coiling O-shapes and spirals on the ripples that moved across the Bay. "O how slow a word is 'rapidly' to express the Life and time-mocking Motion of that Change, always O's before, always Spirals, coiling, uncoiling, *being*".

It was midnight before he went down to the cabin on that Monday night, and wrote in his journal "And what will happen, and whether I shall awake, alive to record what will happen, on Tuesday April 24th, who on earth can tell? Note the superstitious trick of baffling or appeasing possible Evil by a feeling and expression of forced Fear, and encouraged Boding". He was dismayed by the collapse of his new sense of well-being, just when the second part of the voyage was due to start, for the *Speedwell* was expected to sail for Malta next day.

The departure was after all delayed for another day, and on Tuesday morning Coleridge walked to Europa Point with Major Adye, and paid another visit to St Michael's Cave. Adye was an able man, an authority on gunnery, and Coleridge found him congenial and interesting. His local knowledge gave Coleridge new lights on the political situation in the Mediterranean, and they had an instructive talk as they climbed up and down the Rock. The foreboding which Coleridge had felt the night before was horribly relevant to Adye, whatever it was to Coleridge himself. Six months later, Adye died of plague.

Part II

❦

Vanishing Hope

The *Speedwell* and her convoy sailed from Gibraltar at half past ten on Wednesday morning. She nearly came to grief before the start. There was a good deal of confusion with so many ships getting under way in the Bay. One large merchant ship, whose captain was still on shore, was badly handled by her crew when getting under way, nearly collided with three other ships, and then all but hit the *Speedwell* amidships. If Captain Findlay had not shouted directions to her crew, she would have rammed the *Speedwell*, half her size, and inevitably have sunk her. With Findlay's help, the other ship managed just to pass alongside the *Speedwell* without touching her. Coleridge, who was on deck and saw it all, said that the other ship was so close that he could have knocked a shuttlecock on to her forecastle. When it was all over, he and Findlay and the mate Edridge confessed to each other that their knees had trembled at such a narrow escape. "What a death for an old hardy skilful Mariner, to be run down while at anchor by a set of Lubbers!" noted Coleridge in his journal, probably repeating in bowdlerized form one of Captain Findlay's observations on the unskilful crew.

The *Leviathan* was no longer with Coleridge's convoy. Two days earlier she had sailed from Gibraltar to join Nelson's squadron off Toulon, taking with her the bomb ships *Acheron*, *Thunder* and *Etna*, the collier *Harmony* which had come out from Portsmouth with coals for Nelson's ships, and another convoy which had assembled at Gibraltar to wait for an escort along the Spanish coast. When Captain Bayntun arrived at Gibraltar in the *Leviathan*, he found there three frigates, *Medusa*, *Amphion* and *Maidstone*, as well as the sloops which were based on Gibraltar to patrol the Straits. Bayntun decided to send the *Maidstone* to escort the Malta-bound section of the convoy he had brought from England, an arrangement which much annoyed Nelson when he heard of it, as he had already ordered another ship to Gibraltar to collect the eastbound convoy there, and Bayntun's decision upset his carefully-worked-out plans for the movements of his ships.

The *Maidstone* had spent most of the spring cruising off Cadiz with the other two frigates, keeping a watch on the French warship *L'Aigle* which had taken refuge there. It had been a stormy spring, and the *Maidstone* had been much battered, so that her captain had to have her bows lashed in with rope, and keeping her on station at all was a praiseworthy feat. In early April Nelson wrote to Captain Gore, of the *Medusa*, who was in command of the little squadron of frigates, that he was "exceedingly pleased with Captain Elliot's conduct and exertions in keeping the sea with the Maidstone in her present bad state, and request you will be so good as to tell him so". He ordered the three frigates to stop their watch on Cadiz and return to Gibraltar to refit, and after that to cruise outside the Straits to protect convoys from privateers. These orders crossed with a despatch from Gore to Nelson, written on 20th April, the day after Coleridge reached Gibraltar, reporting that the three frigates had come into Gibraltar on 16th April, after sustaining severe damage in a gale off Cadiz the day before, and that the *Maidstone* was anchored off the head of the New Mole at Gibraltar, so that from the Straits she would look ready to go to sea at any moment to drive away privateers; but actually she was waiting her turn for repairs, after the sloop *Halcyon*. (Plate VI i). By the time Nelson's orders arrived in Gibraltar, Bayntun had sent the *Maidstone* off to Malta.

She had had a busy nine days at Gibraltar, taking on water, coals, wood, beef and carpenter's stores, having her bowsprit and foremast refitted, her sails repaired, her rigging set up again. She was a fifth-rate, with a complement of 240 men—201 seamen, 15 volunteers and boys, 24 marines. She was a 32-gun ship, with a single row of gun-ports along her rather ungainly hull. (Plate VI ii). Her captain, when he first saw her, considered her a "remarkably ugly ship, upright stem and stern, and rising very much in the after part of the quarter deck". He added characteristically "As this did not suit a young captain's ideas, I set about altering and beautifying her".

Captain the Hon. George Elliot, Captain of the *Maidstone*, was still under twenty, and had been at sea for ten years. He was a lieutenant at sixteen, a commander at eighteen. This was not entirely due to sheer unaided merit. His father, who was later to be Viceroy of India and Earl of Minto, was a friend of Nelson's. Elliot was later to insist that his successful career in the Navy was not due to family interest, but to his own services and to the help of naval friends. What now seems astonishingly early promotion was not so unusual then; the Navy was so short of officers that every midshipman became a lieutenant on the very day he became eligible, which he did by passing a very easy examination and producing a certificate that he was twenty-one years old. Elliot himself was just sixteen when he produced his copy of this document, which he bought from the hall porter at the Admiralty for five shillings. Perhaps Jane Austen's Henry Crawford exaggerated his exertions to get Fanny Price's brother William made a lieutenant; was there really any need for the string-pulling through his uncle the Admiral, and his uncle's friend Sir Charles, and Sir Charles's friend the First Lord of the Admiralty, by which Henry hoped to buy Fanny's gratitude and love?

George Elliot would probably have had early promotion and a successful career even without influence, and even at a time when officers were not in short supply. He was a brave and able man, but not a lovable one, as he was extremely pleased with himself and very critical of most of his contemporaries, usually because of some ill turn which he thought they had done him. He had a rather cruel sense of humour, which spared nobody whom he considered dull or vulgar or over-cautious, or even just old. He was an efficient commanding officer, and claimed that he had never had any difficulty with any officer or man under him, none of whom had ever been court-martialled.

He had come out with Nelson in the *Victory* in 1803 to join the Mediterranean Fleet. It was a last-minute appointment, of which he heard by a letter from Lord St Vincent which reached him when he was at a ball in London, giving him only till daylight to get to Portsmouth before the *Victory* sailed. He made it, rushing first to Arlington Street to commandeer some of his father's clothes—his own were in the country—and then tearing down to Portsmouth in a post chaise, bribing the postboys to drive at headlong speed. Finding that the *Victory* would after all not sail till the evening, he had a uniform cut out and pinned up in a Portsmouth shop so that it could be finished en route by the *Victory*'s marine tailors; so he was in proper uniform, not still in civilian evening dress, by the time the *Victory* reached the Mediterranean. There he was appointed to command the sloop *Termagant*, superseding her acting captain, an old Scotsman of sixty who was so angry at being made to give way to a boy of eighteen that he refused to sell his crockery and cutlery to his successor as was customary, and Elliot had to collect plates, knives and table-cloths from his friends in the Mediterranean Fleet. He had little sympathy for the elderly officer whom he had displaced. "The old man's name was *Fife*, but he was known as *Old Music*, though at the moment he was certainly very much out of tune". A few months later, on his nineteenth birthday, Elliot was promoted to command the *Maidstone*, which was sent to join the watch on Cadiz, and very nearly went ashore in Ceuta Bay on the way there; Elliot, needless to say, saved the day by his instinctive foresight. "I had then good reason to suspect, what I soon found was the case, that the master was a downright idiot, and the lieutenant of the watch not much better" was Elliot's comment on this event. It is a little difficult to believe that Elliot was quite so much beloved by his men, and found quite so many friends everywhere, as he claimed when as an old man, now Admiral Sir George Elliot, K.C.B., he wrote his memoirs for his children. But he undoubtedly was efficient; Nelson considered him one of the best officers of his age in the Service, fit to be trusted with any mission and keeping his ship in excellent order and condition. Coleridge's convoy was in capable hands.

The wind was west by north when the convoy left Gibraltar, and the *Speedwell* soon began to roll again. After nearly a week in harbour and on shore, Coleridge had lost his sea legs, and was sick after dinner. His malaise was increased by the foul stench of the bilge which suddenly pervaded the ship. In spite of his queasiness, his insatiable scientific curiosity noted chemical reactions all over the ship to the exhalation from the bilge. Gold paint turned red, silver paint brownish-black, ordinary paint a greasy silver where it was clean, reddish-brown where it was dirty, and the red paint of lettering on sacks turned dove-coloured. This seemed so strange to Coleridge that he made notes to ask Humphry Davy to explain the chemistry of these colour changes.

To avoid danger from Algerine pirates, the convoy kept fairly close to the Spanish coast. On Wednesday afternoon and night, while Coleridge dozed fitfully in his bunk with the stink of the bilge in his nostrils, the convoy made good progress with a continuing north-westerly wind, and when he came up on deck on Thursday morning, the snowy peaks of the Sierra de Nevada were in sight. They were the highest mountains he had so far seen on this voyage, but they did not much impress him, and he came to the conclusion that sublimity in Nature was unconnected with mere height and size.

The convoy drove on, past Cabo di Gata; signals poured out from the *Maidstone* to the other ships—Captain Elliot was getting things squared up to his liking. The current "Regulations and Instructions Relating to His Majesty's Service at Sea" laid down, in the chapter on convoys, that "When a Captain is ordered to Convoy Ships from one Port to another, he is to apply to the Commissioners of the Navy, or to the Commissioner at the Port, if there be one, for a sufficient number of printed Convoy Instructions, if he has them not on board, and after filling up the blanks, appointing proper rendezvous, and adding such further Signals and Instructions as circumstances may require, he is to deliver one, signed by himself, to each of the Masters of Ships or Vessels put under his protection; strictly charging him to keep it in his own possession; and not to inform any person whatever of the rendezvous or secret signals appointed in it". No copy of these special convoy instructions seems now to be extant, but the current "Signal Book for the Ships of War" has a section for signals to and from merchant ships. These include signals for the escort to direct merchant ships to close nearer or open to a greater distance, and to make or shorten sail, and other signals for the merchant ships to indicate to their escort ship various difficulties, distresses and needs for assistance. The *Speedwell* was going to need one of these before long.

On Thursday afternoon the favourable wind began to die down, and in the next few days the convoy made little progress. On Friday morning there was almost a dead calm, and what breezes there were began to shift to the east. Coleridge was on deck with Captain Findlay, who suddenly noticed a bright golden spot on the water. It was a hawk's-bill turtle, and at once the ship was in a turmoil of the hunting instinct. "With all the whole Sailor's whole Bustle and Bellow, and Life and Death Impatience, rapid, loud, eager, passionate Command, vehement reiteration, abrupt Transition, every the lightest order conveyed in the form of Reproach and Abuse, with Oaths intermixed, like the Stars that start up, sparkle, dart flames and die away in the Snow of Foam by the vessel's side", Captain Findlay ordered a boat to be launched. He and Coleridge got into it, the Swedish seaman rowed them in pursuit of the turtle, and Findlay leant with out-stretched arms over the bows of the boat as it came quietly up beside the sleeping turtle and he was able to seize it by the tail and bear it back in triumph to the *Speedwell*. Coleridge felt sorry for the strange-looking parrot-beaked creature as it lay sighing on its back on the deck, beating its breast feebly with its fore flippers. However he sallied out again in the boat with Findlay and the Swede, looking for more turtles while the *Speedwell* lay becalmed, and exhausted himself in the hot noonday sunshine by helping to bail the boat as it circled round, looking for more turtles and trailing a bait of an orange and a dead sea-bird. But the other turtles were wary, waking and plunging instantly before the boat could get near them, and Captain Findlay caught no more, though later during dinner there was another "turtle alarm" and the mate, Edridge, went out in a boat and caught a large one. Coleridge, who had already heard a lot about the different kinds of turtle from Findlay's repetitive conversation, was interested to see the odd creatures in action. It was a day of sea creatures; at one time the water was alive with leaping bonitos, and there were schools of porpoises shooting through the sea "with a noise of rushing, like that of a vessel dashing on by steam or other power within itself, thro' the Calm, and making the Billows and the Breeze, which it did not find". Such sounds, far-heard across the sea, carried him back into the world of the Ancient Mariner. The day had been full of such reminiscences, from the skeletal profiles of the distant becalmed ships around the *Speedwell* to the seamen's stories of birds like the albatross which never come to land for years, but live and sleep on the sea.

Captain Findlay's furious bustle over the turtle hunt amused Coleridge. Findlay had turned out not to be the mild quiet man that Coleridge had taken him for at first. He was hardy, skilful and weather-wise, but passionate and impatient, superstitious, slangy, foul-mouthed and a heavy drinker. He evidently liked Coleridge, and they had many long conversations, and also some drinking-bouts. On this Friday evening Coleridge, who had spent the afternoon having a siesta to rest his aching back after the morning's energetic bailing, was up on deck again till midnight, pacing up and down. Captain Findlay invited him to have some rum grog, which he imprudently accepted, and was instantly sick. "Surely, I shall not be so contemptibly weak as ever to do this again!" wrote Coleridge; but of course he was.

XX· Friday 27th April

Coleridge's mind lived on several different planes at once. While he was leaning on the *Speedwell*'s nettings and listening to Captain Findlay's sputter of oaths as he ordered out the boat for the turtle hunt, Coleridge was also looking at the sea below him, noticing the sun-sparkles among the foam of the wake, and conflating in a metaphor the observations of his eyes and of his ears. Everything he saw was liable to cross into the realm of allegory, specially if it was a natural phenomenon of light and colour. He and Tom Wedgwood had been studying such phenomena together for years, Humphry

Davy's chemistry lectures had stimulated his interest still more, and one of his projects was for a series of Hymns to the Sun, Moon, Air, Fire and Water, which would have netted the patterns of moving light on which he had gazed so long and intently.

From the deck of the *Speedwell* he could see the reflection cast by the sun through the sails and rigging onto the sea. It looked like "a Vase or a circular Plume of flames in tortuous flakes of bright sulphur-blue; cherubic swords of Fire—now blowing all one way, now dividing, now blossoming in a complete crater-vase (a lily flower!)". In the centre of this burning blue crater he could see the shadow of his own head and torso as he leant over the side of the ship. The shadow of his shoulders and arms massed into a shape like a mountain, and when he stretched out his arm, the shadow was like a dim flake of cloud stretching out from the mountain across the sky-like blue of the sunlit sea. Round the shadow of his head there was a halo of radiance, a Glory.

The Glory was one of the most cherished images of the Romantic writers. James Hogg introduced it at a crucial moment in *Confessions of a Justified Sinner*, and it was one of De Quincey's master images in *Suspiria de Profundis*, where he made it stand for a reflex from man's inner nature, a projection into consciousness of hidden unrecognized emotions.

The expression "Glory" as used by Coleridge and his contemporaries covered several different types of ocular spectra. The most celebrated was the vision known as the Spectre of the Brocken. (Plate VII i). This legendary giant of the Harz Mountains has actually been photographed in our own day by Mr F. S. Smythe. A huge shadowy head and shoulders, seen in profile, float in mid-air above the jagged mountain-top, which is black against the lightening dawn sky; and round the head is a triple aureole, light, then dark, then light again. It was well known in Coleridge's day that the Spectre could be seen by a climber on the top of the Brocken, when the sun was low and cast the climber's shadow on to a layer of mist. What he saw on the mist spread before him in space was a huge figure, and round its head was a corona of vivid colours like the haloes of saints in early Flemish paintings. Most of us when travel-

VII   The Glory
        (i)   The Spectre of the Brocken (*above*)
        (ii) The Glory seen by John Haygarth near the Vale of Clwyd (*below*)

VIII   "The Ship drove fast, loud roared the blast,
And southward aye we fled". *Illustration by Gustave Doré to* The Ancient Mariner

ling by air have seen such a glory surrounding the shadow of the aeroplane on the clouds below us. The vision is thought to be caused by scattered refraction of the sun's rays from drops of water in the mist, but no one knows for certain.

The Spectre of the Brocken was not often seen, as the angle of the sun and the atmospheric conditions had to be just right; the early morning was the most propitious time, and it took some exertion to reach the distant summit of the Brocken by daybreak. Coleridge himself never saw it, though he twice climbed the Brocken when he was in Germany in 1799, and made careful notes of descriptions by German naturalists of their sightings of the Spectre. The giant haunted his imagination ever afterwards, though he may not have known one fact about this vision which made it perfectly allegorical for his own purposes. If several men are on the mountain top together, each can see his own shadow and the shadows of the others, but each man sees the glory only round his own head, not round the others'.

It was not only on the Brocken that the Glory was seen. The airy cities and armies of the Fata Morgana which hung over the sea off Messina were another such vision which entranced Coleridge's imagination, and there were shy phantoms nearer home. As early as 1798, Coleridge's eye had been caught by a description in a Manchester scientific journal of a Glory observed by a traveller in the Welsh hills at sunset, who had seen his own shadow projected onto a band of white mist, with a halo round its head coloured in the sequence of the rainbow, with red outermost, and arched over at a distance by a shining white bow. The traveller, Haygarth, recorded that "it resembled, very exactly, what in pictures is termed a *glory*, around the head of our Saviour, and of saints: not indeed that luminous radiance, which is painted close to the head, but an arch of concentric colours, which is placed separate and distinct from it". This exciting description was accompanied by a stiff little engraving (Plate VII ii) which nevertheless has its own ghostly *frisson* too, and it caught Coleridge's fancy for life. Many years later he claimed to have twice seen the same phenomenon "which occurs occasionally when the air is filled with fine particles of frozen Snow,

I

constituting an almost invisibly subtle snow-mist, and a Person is walking with the Sun behind his Back". Coleridge's own two observations of the Glory may possibly have been not the Brocken Bow type, but the more often seen Heiligenschein, which haloes a man's shadow cast on dewy grass in early morning; or the reflection of a tiny sun, haloed in threads and hairs of green and gold light, which he once saw on a glossy leaf; or he may have been referring to his vision, this April morning on the *Speedwell*'s deck, of a third type of Glory, the aureole of light seen round a man's shadow on water. This has often been seen by men standing by, or bathing in, tree-shaded ponds; but according to Minnaert's fascinating *Light and Colour in the Open Air*, a book that Coleridge would have rejoiced in, this phenomenon "can be seen best of all when looking from a bridge or deck of a ship at one's shadow falling on the restless dashing of the waves. Thousands of light and dark lines diverge in all directions from the shadow of our head . . . The rays do not converge precisely at one and the same point but only approximately. Another remarkable thing is the increase in the general brightness in the surroundings of the shadow. Nothing of it is to be seen on calm water or on water with even waves; it can only be seen well when irregular little mounds of water arise from the surface . . . The explanation is that each unevenness in the water's surface casts a streak of light or shade behind it; all these streaks run parallel to the line from the sun to the eye, so that we can see them meet perspectively in the anti-solar point—that is, in the shadow-image of our head". This description perfectly corresponds with the blowing dividing crater of tortuous flame and fiery swords that Coleridge saw.

The shadow with a halo round its head that only the caster of the shadow could see: it was an image from which Coleridge drew more despair than comfort. When he wrote in *Dejection* of

"A light, a glory, a fair luminous cloud"

which came from the soul of the beholder, he was using the legend of the seldom-seen Spectre of the Brocken to express his loss of joy, which had dulled everything he saw, once so haloed with visionary brightness. Poetic genius, one's own or others', can show one the prismatic aureole round the head of the shadow-figures which it creates, and in which one recognizes one's own projection, he was later to say of Shakespeare. The unsophisticated eye may fail to recognize the projection, and may recoil from the shadow as though it were a spectre with a life of its own; but might it not be worse still if one knew it as a projected form of one's own nature to which one's eye had attached a delusive radiance of hope?

Colcridge linked the Glory round his shadow-head which he saw from the deck of the becalmed *Speedwell* with the dream of Sara Hutchinson which ran through all his feelings, and this became the seed of a poem, *Constancy to an Ideal Object*, which he may have actually written down a few months later in Malta. The image of his love was a "yearning Thought", "The only constant in a world of change", but it was an image of vain hopes, never to be fulfilled, an image in his own mind which bore no resemblance to external realities.

"Yet still thou haunt'st me; and though well I see,
She is not thou, and only thou art she,
Still, still as though some dear embodied Good,
Some living Love before my eyes there stood
With answering look a ready ear to lend,
I mourn to thee and say—'Ah! loveliest friend!
That this the meed of all my toils might be,
To have a home, an English home, and thee!'
Vain repetition! Home and Thou are one.
The peacefull'st cot, the moon shall shine upon,
Lulled by the thrush and wakened by the lark,
Without thee were but a becalmed bark,
Whose Helmsman on an ocean waste and wide
Sits mute and pale his mouldering helm beside.

And art thou nothing? Such thou art, as when
The woodman winding westward up the glen
At wintry dawn, where o'er the sheep-track's maze

Friday 27th April

> The viewless snow-mist weaves a glist'ning haze,
> Sees full before him, gliding without tread,
> An image with a glory round its head;
> The enamoured rustic worships its fair hues,
> Nor knows he makes the shadow he pursues!"

When Coleridge made a note about the Glory that he saw that Friday morning, he classified it among "Hints taken from real Facts by exaggeration". Was the Sara of his imagination a distorted exaggeration of the real-life Sara? He spent that evening on deck watching the sunset and the rising of a bright star and of the waning moon, and paced up and down indulging in some sweet thoughts and some melancholy ones. He dreamt of Sara that night, but most of the dreams did not show her true likeness—

"She is not thou, and only thou art she".

The dreams were distorted by doubts and jealousies, which made him increasingly miserable as Friday became Saturday, and Saturday Sunday, and still the convoy made no progress but was held back by capricious and contrary breezes which left the *Speedwell* rolling wretchedly in a sluggish swell.

"Why aren't you here?" his heart had cried to Sara a fortnight earlier, in the buoyant opening days of his voyage. Now he felt as if he could not sustain her actual presence with him during the voyage. He wanted to live with his idea of her, not with her breathing reality. He told himself, when this feeling came over him, that it was because he could not bear to think how Sara, or Dorothy or Mary Wordsworth, would suffer if they had to endure the discomforts and miseries that he was undergoing on this voyage. He tried to fix his mind on philosophical definitions of pain and pleasure, of will and emotion, in general application and not just in his own case— how they might, for instance, be treated in the poem on which Wordsworth was working. But there was a poem of his own that he was beginning to envisage—

"Why are you not here? O no! O no! I dare not wish you here. A poem in two parts".

When he was cheerful and optimistic, he wanted Sara's presence, but when he was sad, when he was ill, there was a movement of his heart as though something closed, and he persuaded himself that he did not want to see her because he did not want her to suffer and sadden too. If she and hers were well and happy, they were better away from him. Beneath this there was a fear, an intuition that he was safer alone with his imagined figure of her than with her real presence. "Well I see, She is not thou". His love was a reality, but the woman on whom it was focused was not really like the image of her that he loved, the dream creature who was all "answering look" and "ready ear", who existed only in relation to him. He had made the shadow he pursued.

XXI · *Saturday 28th April to Wednesday 2nd May*

For the next few days the wind blew steadily from the east and the convoy made little headway. The weather was oppressive, sometimes foggy, at other times there were heavy showers of rain and the sky was overcast, with a heavy flounce of clouds above the horizon, "flannel-petticoated all the way round" Coleridge called it, in a homely simile from his children's nursery, or his own, since little boys as well as little girls wore flannel petticoats then. Denizens of nineteenth-century nurseries, and even of some twentieth-century ones, can remember that flannel petticoats always had scalloped edges, very like the outlines of the cumulus clouds which hung above the horizon round the halted convoy.

As the contrary breezes shifted east-north-east, east-south-east, back to due east, and died down altogether, and began again, signals went out from the *Maidstone* to the convoy to tack, to close up, above all to keep together, and the crew of the *Maidstone* practised their muster to action stations. The convoy's position was dangerous, almost immobilized as they were for days together in the stretch of sea fifty miles south of Cartagena and less than a hundred north of the Algerian coastline. They would be an easy prey for aggressors from either direction, French privateers from the Spanish ports or corsairs from Algiers and Oran. If, in the first part of his voyage, Coleridge gave little thought to the dangers of such a journey in war-time, the news of naval disasters that he had heard at Gibraltar had woken him up, and he was beginning to doubt the advantages of travelling in a convoy. "It is a common notion that going under Convoy you are as snug as a bug in a rug" he wrote to Southey (a surprisingly early use of a modern-sounding piece of slang; probably he had picked it up from the *Speedwell*'s crew). In fact there were many disadvantages. The faster ships were always having to heave to and wait for the slower ones; in calms or in foggy weather the ships were in frequent danger of colliding with each other; and "where Calms are most common a privateering or piratical Row boat might board you and make slaves of you, under the very nose of the Man of War, which would lie a lifeless Hulk on the smooth water". He had heard at Gibraltar of a British frigate which had very nearly been made to strike her colours by privateers, and the convoy's present escort was only a frigate.

His poor state of health increased his gloom. The *Speedwell* was rolling worse than ever in the uneasy Mediterranean swell and the stink from the bilge was terrible. He vomited up all his dinner on Saturday, spent the next twenty-four hours in "unwholesome and painful Dozings" in his bunk, and could eat nothing till Sunday afternoon when he managed to swallow a little rice. On Sunday night, though there was a thunderstorm and a downpour of rain, he slept better—proof that his ailments were not so automatically brought on by bad weather as he was apt to claim. Probably he had ensured a good night's rest by a dose of laudanum.

On Monday morning, though the wind was still contrary, the *Speedwell* was rolling less, and Coleridge was sufficiently recovered to write up his journal and to go on deck and have a gossip with Captain Findlay and the crew. His ignorance of nautical terms and his craving curiosity seem to have amused the crew of the *Speedwell*, who tried to teach him the names of the sails and rigging and how they worked, the meaning of various signals, how the ship's position was calculated, and practical tips about not emptying ashes or scalding water over the windward side.

The Ancient Mariner whose skinny hand tightened more and more on Coleridge's shoulder as the voyage went on, made him listen above all to the sailors' stories of their superstitions—of smelling a wind or whistling for one, of lucky and unlucky days for sailing on, of Jonahs who brought evil fortune to a ship. The contrary wind which held up the ships day after day started talk of a Jonah in the convoy. Coleridge said to himself that for this reason at any rate it was safer to be one of a convoy; "on a single Vessel the Jonas must have been sought out among ourselves". As it was, Captain Findlay decided that their new Commodore, Captain Elliot, was the bringer of ill luck. Coleridge heard him muttering at the *Maidstone*'s slow progress, well equipped as she was. "He has muster enough. Top Sails and top gallant Sails, and Royals—The Devil has helped him to a Commodore's Share. Aye! aye! the Devil knows his relations".

Coleridge noted how the superstitious sailor mind always moves from vexation to reproach and anger, and then attaches its superstitious feelings to the object of its anger, specially when the object controls the sailor's own fate. An idea for an essay on superstition instantly started up in Coleridge's mind. It would begin with the superstitions of savages, peasants, fishermen, gamblers, within a framework of crude religious belief, but it would go on to analyse the less obvious credulity of those who "have no religion or only what is called an entirely rational one, and who from infancy have been taught to derive a self-importance from Contempt of and (supposed) Insight into all the common forms and conventional outlets of Superstition", but who nevertheless have "subtle Incarnations and Epiphanies" of superstition, which they do not recognize as such.

He was trying to abstract a theory from some feelings of his own, as well as from the old wives' tales of the *Speedwell*'s crew. When he wrote *The Ancient Mariner* he had calculatingly used his insight into common forms of superstition, and even on this voyage he was turning over in his mind some possible variations on the idea of a curse from a waning moon, of ill luck from a star closely dogging the moon, which he had learned from the sailors and intended to use in a future poem, or in a revision of *The Ancient Mariner*. But in Gibraltar he had caught out his own mind indulging in a superstitious trick to avert evil. Since then the foreboding of loss and failure and moral stagnation had been growing on him, not to be stifled by abstract thought, not to be lulled even by recourse to drugs. By Wednesday afternoon he was in bed again and desperately sick, trying one medicine after another to cure the costiveness which renewed opium doses had brought on. Nothing did him any good; he tried turkey rhubarb, which brought him no relief and merely made him bilious. His dreams were becoming more and more strange and distressing, and he was beginning to have hallucinations of vision. In this sick hour, his dream of being re-created by the voyage to the Mediterranean shrivelled. "Tuesday afternoon, one o'clock, May Day. We are very nearly on the spot, where on Friday last about this same Hour we caught the Turtles—And what are 5 days' toiling to Windward just not to lose ground, to almost 5 *years*! Alas! alas! what have I been doing on the Great Voyage of Life since my return from Germany but fretting upon the front of the Wind—well for me if I have indeed kept my ground even!"

The idea of himself that sickened Coleridge most was the image of a becalmed ship. To be a ship crippled by storms of misery—"now mastless, rudderless, shattered,—pulling in the dead swell of a dark and windless Sea", as he had felt three years earlier at a time of illness and domestic strife was bad enough, but still bearable because tragic and noble. But what if the ship is still well-found, with every sail spread, and yet no wind blows to bear her on? Before he started on the voyage to Malta, he had hopefully seen himself as a bark driven on regularly and lightly by a trade wind, and had compared himself and Southey to two ships that left port in company, fit subject for a "divine Allegory". As the voyage lengthened, and as he watched and reluctantly identified with the laggard ships of the convoy, crowded with sail yet unable to profit by the wind and catch up, the divine allegory turned devilish. "My Hopes

—O me! that they which once I had to check should now be an effort. Royals and Studding Sails and the whole Canvas stretched to catch the feeble breeze!" He was falling behind in the great voyage of life, on which others were forging ahead. Six months earlier he had written of Wordsworth as he began to work on *The Prelude*—"Now he is at the Helm of a noble Bark; now he sails right onward—it is all open Ocean, and a steady Breeze; and he drives before it, unfretted by short Tacks, reefing and unreefing the Sails, hauling and disentangling the Ropes". It was a prophetic contrast with Coleridge's own literal and metaphorical condition now, tacking uselessly and making no progress, fretting upon the front of the wind. In the packet of copies of Wordsworth's poems which Coleridge had with him in the *Speedwell* was one sonnet which was well calculated to pain him, though its intention was the opposite.

"Where lies the Land to which yon Ship must go?
Fresh as a lark mounting at break of day,
Festively she puts forth in trim array;
Is she for tropic suns, or polar snow?
What boots the inquiry?—Neither friend nor foe
She cares for; let her travel where she may,
She finds familiar names, a beaten way
Ever before her, and a wind to blow".

Wordsworth's ship was in his own image, not in Coleridge's; that was now an idle ship lagging with limp sails that could not catch the wind.

XXII · *Monday 30th April*

At ten o'clock on the evening of 30th April, when Coleridge's convoy was loitering south-east of Cabo de Palas, Southey's wife gave birth to a daughter at Greta Hall. Southey was not rapturous about his daughter's beauty. He described her ruthlessly as "very, very ugly; so ugly that, if I did not remember tales of my own deformity, how both mother and grandmother cried out against me, notwithstanding my present pulchritude, I should verily think the Edithling would look better in a bottle than on a white sheet. She may mend, and in about three months I may begin to like her, and by and by I suppose I shall love her; but it shall be with a reasonable love, that will hang loosely upon me, like all second loves". He was making a conscious effort to be cool and uninvolved, after the heartbreak when his daughter Margaret died the previous year.

The fine weather had come at last, and the trees which had been bare so long and late that year were now bursting into green along the valleys and the borders of the lakes, and the orchards at Dove Cottage and Greta Hall were budding. The summer season of long walks and expeditions began. Wordsworth walked over to spend three days at Greta Hall, and when he went back to Grasmere, Southey went with him, and from there on to London to do the urgent literary jobs that had been hanging fire while he waited at Keswick for the birth of his child.

Wordsworth told his family when he got home that he had found Mrs Coleridge well and in good spirits, and that the three Coleridge children were also all well. They were an interesting trio, and both their parents doted on them. "If my wife loved me, and I my wife, half as well as we both love our children, I should be the happiest man alive" Coleridge confided to Southey. The children were not models of good behaviour, but their parents found them perfect. When Hartley as a riotous three-year-old gave Godwin a rap on the shins with a ninepin, and Godwin complained to Mrs Coleridge, Hartley's indulgent father commented that he was perhaps rather rough and noisy, but that Godwin's own children were terrorized into a "cadaverous Silence" that was "quite catacomb-ish"; he was not going to have his own children dragooned like that. Instead they led a free but cherished life at Keswick, rushing about inside and outside the house, welcomed and spoiled by all the neighbours, and at home allowed to say what they thought, to ask any questions they liked, which were attended to and answered as though they were grown-ups. They got a reasonable and healthy amount of teasing, too, but their individualities were respected.

In April 1804 Hartley was a brilliant elusive fidgety child of seven. "A strange strange Boy" his father had called him a few months earlier, a boy without vanity, pride or resentment, passionate but never angry, not very affectionate, extremely truthful, wrapped up in metaphysical speculations. "I am always thinking of my Thoughts" he told his father, and his thoughts were on ontological problems: would the mountains always be there? what would it be like if all the visible world vanished, and nothing was left? how many Hartleys were there really? was a madman a man at all? Not only his own father but Southey, Wordsworth, everyone that knew the boy thought he was a genius, so utterly individual that you could never forget him once you had seen him. With all that, he was not an obviously attractive child. He was not much to look at, a small skinny boy with a low forehead. He was idle and backward at ordinary lessons; he loved thinking, but he hated reading and being wise and being good, he told his father. He had wild bursts of excitement and joy, but also strange inconsolable fears. Since everybody at Greta Hall had at least one nickname, given them by Coleridge or Southey, Hartley was known as "Moses".

His younger brother Derwent, three and a half at this time, was much more easy to understand, the conventional model of a fine boy. He was a sturdy handsome broad-chested child, a "cube of fat" his father once called him, nicknamed "Stump" or "Stumpy Canary", because of his square outline and a yellow frock in which he had once appeared, and also "Justiculus" and "the River God" and "Pi-pos Pot-pos", his pronunciation of the "striped opossum" and "spotted opossum" which he used to point out in his animal picture-book. He was a precocious learner who could say all the letters of the alphabet, and recite the names of sixty different animals from their pictures on cards, by the time he was two. But otherwise he was a very normal little boy, affectionate, mischievous and greedy. Southey said that all Hartley's guts were in his brains, and all Derwent's brains in his guts. His father summed him up as "a fat large lovely Boy—in all things but his voice very unlike Hartley—very vain, and much more fond and affectionate—none of his Feelings so profound —in short, he is just what a sensible Father ought to wish for—a fine, healthy, strong, beautiful child, with all his senses and faculties as they ought to be—with no chance, as to his person, of being more than a good-looking man, and as to his mind, no prospect of being more or less than a man of good sense and tolerably *quick parts*".

The Coleridges' youngest child, Sara, was two. She was later to be a sickly child, after a near-drowning in the river Greta, but at this time she was a thriving healthy creature with a fair skin and large blue eyes. Southey called her "Fat Sal", and she was also known as "Sally", as "Sariola", and as "Coleridgiella". She was a contented good-tempered baby, basking in quiet happiness, with a smile like moonlight. "You told me nothing about sweet Sara" Coleridge complained to his wife in a letter written two months before he sailed for Malta. "Tell me everything, send me the very Feel of her sweet Flesh, the very Looks and Motions of that mouth. O I could drive myself mad about her".

Though Coleridge, like all normal fathers, was occasionally irritated by his children's tricks, he was tenderly devoted to them. He worried about their health and their diet, he pondered and planned the best way of forming their minds, he constantly recorded in his letters and notebooks the most detailed observations of their character and growth, he treated all his friends to anecdotes of them, he was never bored by their shouting or disgusted by their ailments. During the voyage to Malta he dreamed about them and prayed for them. His almost sensual rapture about the feel of little Sara's flesh is a startling contrast to Southey's cool jokes about the repulsiveness of his new-born Edithling. In a note made a few days later, Coleridge repeated his contention that a man should be valued for what he is, not for what he does, and referred back to the character-sketch of Southey which he had drawn three months earlier, as a man who, judged by what he did, passed every test, but judged by what he was, failed the most important one. Which would one rather have had as a father, if one had been one of the Greta Hall children—a caressing understanding genius who vanished and left others to pay one's school bills, or an undemonstrative presence, sometimes pompous and obtuse but always kind, who provided emotional and economic security?

XXIII· *Wednesday 2nd May to Monday 7th May*

On Wednesday evening the *Maidstone* and the *Speedwell* were almost within a stone's throw of each other, still held up by the persistent head wind, in a featureless stretch of sea with a dreary bank of fog round the horizon. The *Maidstone*'s crew were dancing on deck to the music of a fiddle. The sound carried across the water to Coleridge on the *Speedwell*'s deck, and then was suddenly broken off as the crew were called from their dancing to shorten sail. Coleridge watched and timed the highly trained crew of the warship as they sprang onto the shrouds at the boatswain's whistle, and swarmed up, ten or twelve to each yard, twenty on the main topsail. Another whistle and the sails dropped down, "with a loud whistle of their own thro' the Ropes and Rigging (O how far louder, and far sweeter and altogether another whistle than that of the Boatswain's which yet is not unpleasant)". The reefs were taken in, the sails set again, and in an instant the shrouds were bare of men. The whole evolution took two minutes—Coleridge timed it by reciting lines of poetry.

The *Maidstone*'s log for next day, Thursday, shows that the convoy had hardly moved in twenty-four hours. The wind was still easterly and fitful and the atmosphere was foggy and oppressive. The sea was no longer the sparkling zircon blue-green colour that Coleridge had seen with such joy in the Atlantic. Under this dull sky it was sombre, like polished steel, except close against the hull of the *Speedwell*, and there it was a deep bright indigo blue, thinning to delicate transparent sky-blue where the ripples of the wake arched to break into bright foam. During these days flocks of little yellow-breasted birds appeared and settled in the ship's rigging, while others, dark and shaped like swallows, skimmed close above the waves. Another merchant ship in the convoy, the *Leopard*, lay close to the *Speedwell*, and her reflection slid and elongated across the oily waves between the two ships.

That Thursday evening the wind dodged restlessly, once shifting right round to the favourable westerly quarter, but only for a few minutes. At half past nine Captain Findlay came down to the cabin and promised that there would be a fair wind next day, and on Friday morning Coleridge jubilantly celebrated Findlay's weather-wisdom in a doggerel poem, for the wind had got into the right quarter at last.

> "A Health to Captain Findlay!
> Bravo! Captain Findlay!
> When we made but ill speed with the Speedwell,
> Neither Poet nor Sheep could feed well . . .
> Bravo! Captain Findlay—
> Foretold a fair wind
> Of a constant mind,
> For he knew which way the Wind lay".

The convoy was now at last making progress across the squally sea south of the Balearic Islands. On Friday they were south-west of Formentera, and by Saturday they were opposite Cabrera, the little island south of Majorca.

Coleridge's energies revived once the ship was really on the move again and he need no longer lament

> "Malta, dear Malta as far off as ever".

He read some of the books he had with him, and made notes on them. He studied his Italian grammar, which annoyed him by its section of lachrymose poems about lovers bewailing cruel mistresses, and amused him by the unlikely collocations of its vocabulary, which under "Accidents and Diseases" listed together a fillip, a cuff, a box on the ear, a kick. Coleridge made up a dialogue which would use them all.

"I met with a run of a sad accident today!"

"What, my dear Sir!"

"Mr — gave me first a cuff, then pulled me by the nose, then gave me a box of the ears and lastly, kicked me!"

It put him in mind of a project he had once had of writing an essay on "the morals and manners of the makers of Dictionaries and Grammars", and this in turn made him think of how one day he might collaborate with Wordsworth, Lamb and Southey to produce a periodical something like the *Spectator*. During this week his mind was full of literary projects: plays about Gibraltar and Malta, political commentaries, essays, and "my voyage in verse"—this last was to be written now, "*adesso*" as he put it, exercising his newly learnt Italian and underlining to fix his own attention on it. But he seems never to have taken action on this, except for his scrap of doggerel about Captain Findlay and a draft of a rude song, to be called *Transpositions! Wonders of Transpositions!*, inspired by the appearance of his fellow passengers. Poor fat Mrs Ireland prompted the first stanza—

"When young, come dancing in on the stage
And O then we sing so pretty,
'The World for a Lass' which we exchange in age
For that doleful ditty
'Alas for the World' ",

while the second stanza celebrated Mr Hastings's pimpled purple countenance and swimming black eyes which

"shine and shine, and as they shine
For ever will shine on,
Till what with Brandy, what with Rum,
The Liver's fairly gone!"

This rollicking sketch for a song ended with a more sombre note, that Hastings's eyes shone as a lighthouse does, not to give themselves light but to show others what to avoid. Coleridge was taking home a warning to himself. This Friday, after eating a hearty dinner, he was tempted by curiosity and philhellene piety to drink some Greek island wine "and instantly my whole dinner was in the sea" he ruefully noted. The effect of this, and of an evening of writing up his journal in a cramped position while the ship was rolling, made him so ill that he had to stay in his bunk, flat on his back on a starvation diet, for the next twenty-four hours. And by Saturday morning the favourable wind had changed again—it was back in the east, and rain was falling heavily.

Coleridge's mood of light-hearted nonsense died with the favourable wind, and a grim tempest blew up, in the outside world and in his mind. On Sunday the convoy was in sight of Majorca, and the Commodore had signalled to alter course southward, when a storm began to blow. Captain Findlay at first ridiculed Coleridge for calling it a storm, and would not even allow him to say that the sea was rough, but by three o'clock that afternoon Findlay admitted that it was a real storm, and at four o'clock the *Speedwell*'s foremast yard was carried away. The fury of the wind and sea was at its height that night; next morning, the *Maidstone*'s log reported "Strong gales with a great sea"; she had sprung her main topsail yard in the violence of the storm. The *Speedwell* was so tossed about that Coleridge stayed in his bunk for sheer safety, it would have been impossible to keep on his feet and not be murderously thrown about. The fetor of the bilge filled the stifling little cabin. Yet neither Coleridge nor Mrs Ireland, prone in their bunks, was seasick, though all the crew except Captain Findlay were. Coleridge dozed, and drank chocolate, and thought about death.

If, at the start of his voyage, his imagination had not been fully open to the dangers he would run, it could not remain closed now, when he thought of what he had heard in Gibraltar: of the *Apollo*'s sailors struggling and sinking in the breakers off Cape Mondego, of the outgunned crew mown down on the deck of the *Swift*, of the four men trapped between decks in the burning *Hindostan* among exploding casks and streams of blazing spirits and suffocating billows of smoke. Now in the *Speedwell* he faced what might happen to him in the next few hours. The danger was probably less great than he thought, but it was his first real storm, and in a cockleshell like the *Speedwell* the wild motion was terrifying. He said to himself that few men's last hours could be more dreadful than this, lying in that cabin waiting to be drowned but not daring to close his eyes, rest his head and compose his mind to resignation, because if he did he would drop into sleep and into dreams more horrible than any waking death could be—frightful dreams of despair in which the individual soul, in a passive extremity of pain, experienced an eternity of damnation, an ever-living Death. The present peril of his body was nothing to that torment of fear. He was calm, and he thought he could remain calm even if all hope of survival were gone, but the horror that sat on his pillow waiting for him in his sleep was an appalling companion for a man facing death.

XXIV · *Saturday 5th May to Tuesday 8th May*

On Saturday morning, when Coleridge was supine in his bunk, sick and sorry for himself in the *Speedwell*'s evil-smelling cabin, William and Dorothy Wordsworth set out for a two-day walk across the Westmorland hills. The weather had relented at last and there was a rush of spring, late-come and exuberant, spreading a mist of brilliant green over the fields and thickets on the valley floors on which they looked down as they climbed over Grisdale Hawes, with Helvellyn looming on their left.

It had been a busy April for the Wordsworth family. Wordsworth had been away for a few days, on a visit to Tom and Sara Hutchinson at Park House, their new farm near Penrith, but for most of the month he had been working strenuously at *The Prelude*; he composed nearly three books of it that April. The work was done out of doors, walking backwards and forwards over and over again on the same stretch of path or field, regardless of time or weather, though when it was really wet he sometimes plodded to and fro under an umbrella. No man ever worried less about looking ridiculous. It was his poetry

K

that mattered, he was oblivious of everything else. He thought that he had the power to contribute to the improvement of mankind, and he was right in thinking so. "It seems a frightful deal to say about one's self" he wrote to a friend on 29th April, describing his poem, "and of course will never be published (during my life time I mean), till another work has been written and published, of sufficient importance to justify me in giving my own history to the world. I pray God to give me life to finish these works which I trust will live and do good".

While Wordsworth did his sentry pace under his umbrella, Dorothy and Mary were busy with household chores, helped for part of the month by Sara Hutchinson who came over from Park House for a visit. Though Mary was still very haggard—"as sadly lean as if she were my twin sister" reported Southey, himself the thinnest of men—her health was better now Johnny had been weaned, and Johnny was certainly none the worse. "My little Boy can crawl about the floor famously and is wondrous stout, with admirable health" reported his father. Johnny's size was a marvel to all the Wordsworths' friends and neighbours; Southey described him as "like the sons of the Anakim" and said that he expected him to walk over from Grasmere to Keswick very shortly.

Wordsworth and Dorothy spent all Saturday crossing the hills, and stayed for the night with friends in Patterdale. Next day in beautiful weather they rode on horseback along the western shore of Ullswater to Lyulph's Tower, and from there walked up to the Aira Force waterfall. Here they parted, Wordsworth going west over the hills to Keswick to stay at Greta Hall, while Dorothy went down again to Ullswater and along its shores to the Hutchinsons' farm. It was Sunday morning, and she met Sara and Tom coming away from Dacre church, and walked back with them to their farmhouse, which she thought looked very pleasant among its brilliant green fields. The Hutchinsons looked well too; Tom, who had had a bad go of rheumatism, was recovering fast with the fine weather, and Sara, though still thin after an illness earlier that spring, was well and cheerful.

Dorothy had come to help Sara settle into the new house, and on

Monday the two young women walked into Penrith to buy house-hold equipment. They walked through the fields and crossed the Dacre brook on stepping-stones, getting their feet wet. It was a day of full spring glory. "Could you but have heard the thrushes and seen the thousand thousand primroses under the trees!" wrote Dorothy, describing her visit in a letter to Lady Beaumont. In the next few days they worked very hard at the farm, putting up beds and making and hanging curtains, but they refreshed themselves by afternoon walks, in weather so fine and warm that they could sit on the grass and look at the shining reaches of Ullswater. One day they visited a friend's empty house by the lake. When they went upstairs, "the view from the window struck upon us both in the same way, as if it were an unearthly sight, a scene of *heavenly* splendour".

It has sometimes been suggested that Dorothy Wordsworth was jealous of Sara Hutchinson because of Coleridge's love for her. The happy companionship of these spring days does not sound like it. Dorothy was thirty-three, Sara twenty-nine; they had lived in the same house for many months together in recent years; their family affections were fixed on the same objects, they were comfortable friends. Later this month, Dorothy described Sara in a letter to Lady Beaumont, in words which are not the ones a jealous woman would have used: "I am pleased to think that when I tell you of this Friend of ours you are prepared with a ready interest for she is one of whom you must have heard Coleridge speak, Miss Sara Hutchinson, one of his most dear and intimate friends, even before she was so nearly connected with us by my Brother's marriage. You will be glad to hear that she is come to be an inhabitant of this country both for his sake and ours, she is fixed at a very sweet place, and seems to be perfectly contented; and pleased with everything around her".

What would Coleridge have thought of Sara's radiant content and good humour at this moment, when he was far away and in danger? He often said that he did not want his sorrows to blight her happi-ness, but he could hardly have been pleased had he heard of quite such carefree enjoyment. Dorothy was thinking of him if Sara was not. In her letters she worried about his health; the Mediterranean climate might work a temporary cure, but when he came back to England he might be just as bad again; certainly he ought not to live permanently in the damp climate of the Lakes. Even in a good climate, he would not recover unless he had tranquillity of mind, and learned to regulate his habits.

Wordsworth in a letter of this time wrote about Coleridge's absence with the perfunctory banality which he considered appropriate in correspondence. Thanking a London friend who had done Coleridge a service before his departure, Wordsworth added: "I am sure nothing could be more grateful to your heart than to be useful to such a Man going upon an errand in which all his friends must be deeply interested. I need not say how much our fireside has suffered upon the melancholy occasion, and what a loss he will be to us". This flatness is no clue to Wordsworth's real feeling towards Coleridge at this time; for that, one must turn to the poem that he was writing. As he strode up and down some sheltered path in the rain, he was always addressing in his mind the friend who had inspired him to write this long work, had conjured him not to waste his powers on minor lyrics but to devote himself to some great task. Again and again he hailed Coleridge in his poem—"O Friend!", "Fellow voyager!", and he wrote as though he were actually talking to Coleridge, explaining where a train of thought had led, arguing, justifying, excusing, defending, as he described his early days in France and his reactions to the French Revolution. It was as though he and Coleridge were walking together in the green dales beside the Rotha or the Derwent, debating about liberty, justice and peace. His mind spoke to Coleridge's across the distance that separated them, revealing his renewal of poetic confidence, the restored courage and hope which had come to him in this "primrose-time" in the midst of his heavy thoughts about Coleridge's departure. Coleridge would understand, as no one but another great poet could, what it was like to feel the wind of inspiration revive and sweep all before it,

> "in such strength
> Of usurpation, in such visitings
> Of awful promise, when the light of sense

Goes out in flashes that have shown to us
The invisible world, doth Greatness make abode.
There harbours whether we be young or old.
Our destiny, our nature and our home
Is with infinitude, and only there;
With hope it is, hope that can never die,
Effort, and expectation, and desire,
And something evermore about to be".

Perhaps Wordsworth's lines, if Coleridge could have heard his voice speaking them then, would have seemed even more cruel than a view of Sara among the primroses, insouciantly happy without him in just such a peaceful cottage, lulled by the song of thrushes, as he had imagined himself dwelling in with her, while he mouldered on a becalmed ship in the waste seas of exile.

XXV· *Monday 7th May to Friday 11th May*

On Monday the gale in which the convoy was caught began to abate, but Coleridge was becoming more and more ill, though not with seasickness. Captain Findlay began to be alarmed about him, and signalled the Commodore to ask if he had a doctor on board the *Maidstone*. "Spoke the Speedwell" records the *Maidstone*'s log, to indicate that a signal had been sent to say that she had on board Sampson Hardy, who had been her surgeon for the last three years. "Mr Hardy, Surgeon of the Maidstone" wrote Coleridge in his journal that day, noting the name in case of urgent need in the near future. The handwriting of the next few entries in his journal is increasingly shaky, some of it illegible, and part of a page has been torn out later, perhaps because his scribblings had become deliriously incoherent. He was now half conscious for much of the time, with strange visual hallucinations floating before his eyes. He saw his own face hanging above him, with the white teeth showing in his ever-open mouth. Flowers in the pattern of the curtains of his bunk expanded into yellow faces, and leaves and tendrils into a woman's head and bust and outstretched arm, which then merged into a great round face formed by the porthole.

His health had been deteriorating since he left Gibraltar. He vomited often, though not from seasickness, and his appetite had quite gone; his breathing was heavy and asthmatic, and his sleep was mostly fitful dozes. But much his worst symptom was constipation, which had now become an agony of discomfort. Doses of the purgative turkey-rhubarb had as usual merely weakened him without doing him any good, and for some days he had stopped taking any aperient. The real cause of his constipation was the opium he had been taking, though he had not yet admitted this to himself. On Tuesday the convoy had begun to cross the stretch of sea between the Balearics and Sardinia, but was making little progress. The heavy swell left by the storm was flattening out, but the wind, which had veered to the west at the end of the storm, was now north-east again and blowing fitfully. "The Sails flapped unquietly, as if restless for the Breeze, with convulsive Snatches for air, like dying Fish" wrote Coleridge, imparting some of his own sensations, as he struggled asthmatically for breath, to the sound of the sails that he could hear as he lay in his bunk.

"Tuesday Night, dreadful Labor, and fruitless Throes, of costiveness" recorded Coleridge, adding fullest details. Next day was a "day of Horror", described with bleak frankness and intensity. "Tried the sitting over hot water in vain. After two long frightful, fruitless struggles, the face convulsed, and the sweat streaming from me like Rain, the Captain proposed to send for the Commodore's Surgeon, and accordingly made sail for the Frigate but by Calm and one thing or other it was late evening before he could speak him. The Surgeon instantly came, went back for Pipe and Syringe and returned and with extreme difficulty and the exertion of his utmost strength injected the latter. Good God!—What a sensation when the obstruction suddenly *shot* up!—I remained still three-quarters of an hour with hot water in a bottle to my belly (for I was desired to retain it as long as I could) with pains and sore uneasinesses, and indescribable desires at length went. O what a time!—equal in pain to any before. Anguish took away all disgust, and I *picked out* the hardened matter and after a while was completely relieved. The poor mate who stood by me all this while had the tears running down his face".

A rumour spread round the convoy that one of the *Speedwell*'s passengers had died, and Coleridge himself expected to die, and was almost happy in the thought. The danger, from septic poisoning in the insanitary conditions of the *Speedwell*, was indeed considerable, in an age before antiseptics. Many people then died from infection after minor and successful treatments and operations. Perhaps what helped to keep Coleridge alive was the ceaseless passion for self-observation which enabled him to write down this startlingly detailed account, only a day after being at death's door. It would have been less startling to his own contemporaries, all of them much more outspoken about these bodily functions than even the most otherwise permissive people generally are today. Coleridge passed on an only slightly less explicit account to his friends in his letters home, and they passed it keenly round; Wordsworth, at second hand from Mrs Coleridge, regaled Sir George Beaumont with the tale of Coleridge's "dangerous constipation, which compelled the Captain to hang out signals of distress to the Commodore for a surgeon to come on board. He was relieved from this at last after undergoing the most excruciating agonies, with the utmost danger of an inflammation of the bowels. All this appears to have been owing to his not having been furnished with proper opening medicines". All the Wordsworth circle kept each other informed in fullest detail about the workings of their bowels; their letters are full of descriptions of costiveness, evacuations, opening medicines—the children's, Sara Hutchinson's, their own.

Coleridge in any case, though he loathed enemas with a "morbid delicacy" which several times made him endanger his life to avoid them, had always been interested in physiology, and as a boy had thought of becoming a doctor like his brother Luke, who allowed him to go round the wards of the London Hospital with him and to hold plasters and watch dressings being done. Then and ever afterwards, Coleridge included medical and surgical books in his enormous reading, and when he was in Germany in 1799 he attended lectures on physiology and anatomy at Göttingen. When he began to be ill himself, his study of his own symptoms was not only a necessary precaution, it was an intellectual excitement. Most of us—who when we are ill, feel nothing but disgust and self-pity, and put the whole experience out of our minds as quickly as possible when we recover —miss the genuine solace and enjoyment of the hypochondriac, for whom the workings of his own body during illness, even the most sordid ones, can be an absorbingly interesting spectacle. No doubt this would have been one of the "Consolations" which Coleridge intended to include in the book which began as an idea for a handbook of mental alleviations for the good sick man.

"I appear to myself like a sick physician, feeling the pang acutely, yet deriving a wonted pleasure from examining its process and developing its causes" he once said. He was speaking metaphorically, but illness, like anything else for him, could become an allegory and was interesting for that reason. Anything, however intrinsically repugnant, could be used as a symbol which would make a poem. A few days after his enema he made this entry in his journal: "Brahman rescuing the Poison Snake sinks into one mass of inorganized Slime! —this for my poem of strange Thoughts and Sights". He had been still more explicit in an early letter where he used bodily function as a paradigm for the working of poetic inspiration: "Your presence, like the Sun, will relax the frost of my genius, and like a cathartic, purify it of all obstructions, so that I expect to flow away in a bloody flux of poetry".

Virginia Woolf, when she was completing a novel, once wrote "The blessed thing is coming to an end, I say to myself with a groan. It's like some prolonged rather painful and yet exciting process of nature, which one desires inexpressibly to have over". It requires some effort not to be disconcerted when writers choose to describe their creative experiences by such metaphors as these.

By Thursday afternoon, Coleridge had sufficiently recovered to go up on deck. The convoy was still almost becalmed, though signals from the Commodore had ordered them to make more sail. The ships were so close together that the sea was patterned with the white reflections of their sails, and the cocks in coops on each ship's deck answered each other's crowing. There had been another turtle hunt, and the *Speedwell*'s crew had caught some large ones. "Fish biting the Barnacles off the Turtle" noted Coleridge, tireless in collecting natural observations. He watched a splendid sunset, rich mulberry red above the horizon, smoky yellow-green above that, and highest of all, the new moon. All next day there was still no favourable wind, and the convoy dipped and balanced in the heavy swell which rolled southward from the Gulf of Lions. Melancholy whistles for a wind went up from the convoy ships, but in the *Maidstone* they were too busy for that—they were repairing the main topsail yard which had been sprung in the storm. A little before sunset a light breeze sprang up, and the convoy moved on at about four knots.

Coleridge was still feverish and languid. He felt that he ought to bring his mind to bear on considering and investigating the real state of his health. "A Warning!" he had written at the end of his account of the enema; he could no longer push away the recognition of what had caused his illness. It was something apart from the rheumatism or gout which was his official complaint. That was painful but quite bearable, because there was no shame or horror attached to it, he could speak of it to all the world. The other illness —"the dull quasi finger-pressure on the Liver, the endless Flatulence, the frightful constipation when the dead Filth *impales* the lower Gut—to weep and sweat and moan and scream for the parturience of an excrement with such pangs and such convulsions as a woman with an Infant"—that had a different cause, one involved in lies and self-deceptions, and a craving for a stimulus which his will was too weak to subdue. But he slid the thought of it away again, for a few more days. This was not yet the time for the "aweful duty" of facing his temptation; not yet, not here, when he was a sick man, voyaging wearily across a barren sea, and there was no congenial mind near him with whom he could discuss it. He would think of it later, when he got to Malta.

XXVI· Friday 11th May to Monday 14th May

Two hundred miles north-east of the convoy, Nelson in the *Victory* was entering the Sardinian harbour of Maddalena on the morning of Friday 11th. The roadstead between the Maddalena Islands and the mainland was full of ships at anchor, most of the Mediterranean Fleet was there: eight ships of the line besides *Victory*, and some sloops, bomb ships and tenders. Only four small ships, frigates and sloops, had been left to keep the watch on Toulon, while the Fleet took on wood and water in Sardinia.

Nelson called the harbour at Maddalena "Agincourt Sound", after the ship whose captain had found and charted this admirable base for the British ships watching Toulon. It was at the north-east corner of Sardinia, just east of the Straits of Bonifacio, a strategic centre for operations in the Gulf of Lions, within reach of Naples, Sicily, Malta and the Spanish coast. Sardinian ports were open to British ships, as the King of Sardinia was an ally—his Piedmontese territory had been occupied by the French. Agincourt Sound had the great advantage of having two entrances, so that the ships could get in and out in whatever quarter the wind stood. It was a windy region, and the Sardinian coast was malarial, but it was a plentiful source of supplies of meat, fish and fruit, and altogether Agincourt Sound was an invaluable asset to Nelson.

One of the 74-guns in the Sound that Friday morning was the *Leviathan*. She had joined *Victory* and the Fleet at sea the day before; like Coleridge's convoy she had been held up by contrary winds since leaving Gibraltar—it had taken her seventeen days to reach the rendezvous with the Fleet. As she idled en route in the fitful calms, her commanding officer, Captain Bayntun, turned his attention to matters of discipline for which there had not been time on the rapid passage between Portsmouth and Gibraltar. Robert Clark and John McCabe, seamen, were given twenty-four lashes each for drunkenness, and Edward Moran forty-eight lashes for theft; a few days later he got another twelve lashes for theft, and David Grogan got six for neglect of duty. The scale of punishment for different offences seems as strange as the punishment itself was grim. It was not exceptionally severe in the *Leviathan*; in the *Maidstone* too, after she reached Malta, five seamen were given twenty-four lashes each for drunkenness. Life between decks in these beautiful ships is almost unimaginable now. Many of the men were there against their will, they had been captured by the press-gangs. They slept and ate in a great dark space so low that no one over about five foot eight could stand upright. In the Mediterranean Fleet their food was slightly more varied than in most warships, and they got a liberal daily allowance of spirits or wine, which accounts for the punishments for drunkenness but makes their savagery even more unjust. The seamen's health was watched, and they got reasonable medical care by the standards of the day, but the weakly had not much chance of survival. The *Leviathan*'s log notes that a boy, John Callaghan, died and was buried at sea on the way to Sardinia.

When the *Leviathan* met the Fleet, a boat was sent for Captain Bayntun to report to Nelson in the *Victory*. He seems not to have revealed to Nelson that he had sent the *Maidstone* to Malta, as Nelson was still writing some days later to Gore on the assumption that the *Maidstone* was at Gibraltar. When Nelson finally heard that she had been sent to Malta, he was incensed; it had upset all his arrangements, since he had already sent the *Agincourt* to Gibraltar to collect that particular convoy. "The going on in the routine of a station, if interrupted, is like stopping a watch—the whole machine gets wrong" he grumbled. He was also displeased to discover that the Master of the collier *Harmony*, which had come out from Portsmouth to Gibraltar with Coleridge's convoy and then joined the Fleet under *Leviathan*'s escort, had managed to defraud all the warships at Maddalena by delivering only partly filled baskets of coal. It was on minor irritations of administration such as this that Nelson had to spend so much of his time reading and dictating letters. He kept an eye on every detail in the life of the Fleet, but they did not distract him from concentration on the larger issues at this critical moment of thc war in thc Mcditerranean.

Packets of letters and despatches reached him when the *Victory* arrived in Agincourt Sound, and in the next few days he dictated a pile of replies. Rumours had reached him that Napoleon was to divorce his wife and marry a German royalty, and that he was likely to be proclaimed Emperor; this last event actually took place within a week of Nelson's letter about it. Napoleon's power over Europe was steadily growing, and it was probable that Spain would enter the war on the side of France. Nelson had no fears that this would seriously affect the balance of power in the Mediterranean, and it would provide rich financial opportunities for his Fleet, since Spanish ships could then be taken as prizes, but "I want not riches at such a dreadful price; Peace for our Country is all I wish to fight for,—I mean, of course, an honourable one, without which, it cannot be a secure one". He had no wish to prey on the wretched Spaniards, who were most reluctant anyway to be drawn into the war; but he longed for the confrontation with the French which had been the object of all his manœuvres for the past year. The French Fleet was still in Toulon; some frigates had sallied out briefly in early April, but their ten ships of the line were still snugly out of reach in harbour. Obviously they were being held back for some definite purpose, probably a rendezvous with the Spanish Fleet if Spain came into the war, and then a rush out into the Atlantic to join in a French invasion of England. "The French I am satisfied have an object in view, and the longer it is deferred the nearer must be its attempt at accomplishing it; some day we shall have them, and then we must try and make them make us amends for all our toils" wrote Nelson on 14th May. "I am, in my Command, deriving as much pleasure as a man can do who is always at sea, for the health and cheerfulness of every individual in this Fleet cannot be exceeded".

"Health and cheerfulness" do not quite apply to the body of young John Callaghan, tumbling about in the Mediterranean rollers, or to Edward Moran whose back had been laid open by sixty lashes in the last few days, but Nelson's men were certainly better cared for and in better heart than elsewhere in the Navy. It was only seven years since the mutinies at Spithead and the Nore, and every commanding officer was watching the morale and discipline of his men with a vigilant eye.

On that Monday Nelson also wrote to Alexander Ball, Governor of Malta, passing on warnings from the British Ambassador in Naples that the pro-British Prime Minister there might be sacked under French pressure, and that the French might be going to attack Malta. "The French papers say, they have more friends in that Island than we think. Great events are certainly near, and I only hope they will tend to give a secure, and of course honourable, Peace".

Coleridge may have read this letter of Nelson's when he became Alexander Ball's secretary in Malta a few weeks later. What he learned from Ball about Nelson gave him a lasting sympathy for Nelson's personality and for what he had endured through the wearisome unrewarding months of the Toulon watch. He knew from Ball that Nelson's temper could be irritable and uneven, but also that he was totally devoted to the interests of the Navy and of his own squadron, towards which "his affections were as strong and ardent as those of a Lover", and that his affection was returned by the enthusiastic devotion of all ranks in the Fleet. Ball also told Coleridge a good deal about Nelson's wife and mistress, both of whom Ball much disliked; Lady Nelson was an intolerable nagger— a piece of gossip which may have quickened Coleridge's fellow-feeling for Nelson.

If De Quincey is to be believed, Coleridge met Lady Hamilton at a party in London years later, in 1812, and so fascinated her by his brilliant conversation that as a tribute to him she performed a scene from *Macbeth*, with such splendour that her performance as Lady Macbeth rivalled that of Mrs Siddons. De Quincey said that Emma Hamilton had "Medea's beauty—and Medea's power of enchantment" and he believed that her friendship with Nelson was perfectly virtuous. De Quincey was writing more than twenty years after the event, over which his memory cast an improbably rosy haze. He remembered Emma Hamilton as one of the two most effectively brilliant women he had ever met, but in 1812 she was a blowsy complaining woman of almost fifty, living a hand-to-mouth life pursued by creditors, though perhaps even then some shreds of the spell could still work.

If Coleridge ever did meet her, he was less credulous than De Quincey, but his comment on the whole story is robust and sensible. "In the name of God, what have we to do with Lord Nelson's Mistresses or domestic Quarrels? . . . To the same enthusiastic sensibilities which made a fool of him with regard to his Emma, his Country owed the victories of the Nile, Copenhagen and Trafalgar".

XXVII· *Saturday 12th May to Sunday 13th May*

Coleridge was convalescent by Saturday, but still feverish at nights, and sleeping badly. Such sleep as he got was only in short snatches, and he had such bad dreams that he screamed in his sleep, and "good Mrs Ireland", as the fat passenger had now become in his estimation, had to wake him up out of these paroxysms. In the early mornings he slept more heavily, without the nightmares but with dreams still gloomy and distressing enough to hang heavy on his spirits during the day. All the same, he was recovering, and had intervals of something more like well-being, a mood in which images and deductions drifted through his mind on waves of reverie, as he sat on deck while the faint but favourable breeze from the north wafted the convoy towards the southerly tip of Sardinia, whose ridges and island-fringed coastline they sighted on Sunday afternoon.

A hawk, which had flown out to sea from that distant blue coast, settled exhausted on the bowsprit of the *Speedwell*, and sat there ruffling its feathers, not moving even when one of the crew shot at it. After more shots, it wheeled off in a gyre, its wings catching the light as it plummeted from a cloud shadow into a shaft of sunlight, and then came back to the *Speedwell*. But there was no rest for it there, the sailors shot at it again, and it flew away to another ship in the convoy. Coleridge heard sailors firing at it from the other ships too, all through the day, and though none of them hit the bird, he thought it must have died of fatigue or drowned as it tried to rest on the water. "O Strange Lust of Murder in Man!—It is not cruelty, it is mere non-feeling from non-thinking" he wrote. His identification was transferring itself from the Mariner to the bird that the Mariner shot, circling in narrowing gyres through sunlight and cloud, downwards and inwards to a waiting death of the heart.

This half-realized image gave him a certain artistic pleasure, enough to set his mind off on a lazy exploration of the aesthetic theories that were always floating suspended in his thought, and hooking themselves onto his visual impressions. Ten days earlier he had seen a light low in the night sky, bright but distant, and had been uncertain whether it was a star or the lantern on the *Maidstone*'s main-top, the special light which commodores of convoys always carried. He had said to himself then that the sublimity which the beholder felt at the sight of this light across the dark sea did not depend on whether or not it was really a star, or only seemed so. On this Saturday evening he saw the light again. He was on deck watching the crescent moon with the old one in its arms, and the evening star close to its upper horn, sinking down towards the horizon, turning redder and more dusky as they sank, while to the east at the head of the convoy the signal light on the *Maidstone*'s topmast shone like another star. He began a train of thought: there is an inherent sublimity in the great beauties of Nature—the moon and stars, thunder, lightning, the Northern Lights—and if a masthead light is taken for a star, or a cart rumbling under a gateway is heard as thunder, the sight and sound in themselves are as genuinely sublime as the ones for which they were mistaken, and no subsequent discovery of their real and banal origins can impair the original experience of sublimity. The sublime does not depend for its effect on mere size—the mountains of Granada were less sublime than other lesser hills—or on associations with danger, such as thunder has; it is felt when the self that perceives it is aware through it of the essential unity of Nature.

The ideas darted through Coleridge's mind like fishes, in half-formed sentences and floating hints—"O there are Truths below the Surface in the subject of Sympathy", "*Ego*, its metaphysical Sublimity—and intimate Synthesis with the principle of Co-adunation"—but there was no one near him to whom he could talk about them, who would understand and fix his darting thoughts. "Oh! dear Friends did you see the crescent with its phantom moon, and the evening Star almost crowning its upper Tip!" he wrote, in a yearning invocation to the family at Grasmere who might be looking this very hour at that same night sky. Wordsworth would grasp the elusive argument about sublimity that Coleridge was trying to formulate, and not only grasp it, but take it up and develop it in his own poetry, as he had so often done before with ideas evolved in talk with Coleridge. The thoughts on sublimity might form part of the great philosophical poem on Man, Nature and Human Life, to which the autobiographical poem which Wordsworth was now writing was to be a Prelude. Coleridge resolved to write to Wordsworth suggesting this.

But first he still had to read the five completed books of Wordsworth's *Prelude* which he had brought with him in the copies made for him by Dorothy and Mary. On Sunday evening, when the *Speedwell* was bowling along at six knots with a fair wind, and Coleridge was feeling well and cheerful in spite of the rolling of the ship, he at last tackled the long-delayed job of reading the poem, about which Wordsworth was so anxiously awaiting his opinion. Coleridge had with him in the *Speedwell* the letter he had received from Wordsworth before he left Portsmouth, in which Wordsworth had said that he would give three-fourths of his possessions to have Coleridge's comments on what he had written. Coleridge had glanced at *The Prelude* and the other Wordsworth manuscripts in his desk at intervals during the voyage, but he had never fully applied his mind to the task of criticism.

Nor did he succeed in doing so now. "I have been trying to read W. Wordsworth's Poem on the Formation of his mind, but I have not been able to deliver myself up to it" he noted later in the evening. It was a failure that struck very cold. *The Prelude* was dedicated and addressed to him, for the Wordsworths at this time its only name was "the Poem to Coleridge". Out of a deep and humble veneration for his friend's genius, Coleridge had urged Wordsworth to bend all his powers to this great work. Wordsworth was a giant, a heaven-sent genius, "the only man to whom at all times and in all modes of excellence I feel myself inferior", Coleridge had generously admitted. Wordsworth had shown him what true poetry was, and from that he had realized that he himself was no true poet. Whatever doubts he might have begun to entertain about Wordsworth's want of sympathy for anyone but his immediate family, Coleridge had never yet doubted that Wordsworth was a great poet.

All the same, he could not now deliver himself up to the poem by Wordsworth which he had inspired, and which he had entreated Dorothy and Mary to copy for him, to be a treasure and an "inspiring Deity" to him in his exile. Whether he ever did read the five books of *The Prelude* while he was in the Mediterranean, will never be known for certain. He said that he had, and had written the comments which Wordsworth so much wanted, and entrusted them to Major Adye when he visited Malta that summer, for transmission home; but all Adye's possessions, including any papers of Coleridge's that he had with him, were burnt when Adye died of plague. Perhaps Coleridge did read Wordsworth's poem in Malta, though he could not read it while he was still at sea; but its full impact did not reach him till nearly three years later, when he was staying at Coleorton with the Wordsworths and Sara Hutchinson, and in a series of evening sessions Wordsworth read aloud the whole of *The Prelude*.

To Coleridge, as he sat evening after evening, surrounded by "All whom I deepliest love—in one room all!", listening to the Orphic music of Wordsworth's great poem, it was an experience of ecstasy and pain, and when the last lines had been read, he spent most of the night in drafting a magnanimous tribute to his friend's achievement. To describe the effect of the poem on him, he went back to his voyage to Malta for sea images of the sparkles in the foam of the wake, the moon reflections on the glassy Mediterranean swell.

> "My soul lay passive, by thy various strain
> Driven as in surges now beneath the stars,
> With momentary stars of my own birth,
> Fair constellated foam, still darting off
> Into the darkness; now a tranquil sea,
> Outspread and bright, yet swelling to the moon".

The stars which lit up in Coleridge's own poetic imagination as he listened were only momentary, they darted off to die in darkness. When he heard *The Prelude*, Coleridge was pierced with despair as well as admiration, with a sickness of heart at the inevitable comparison with his own lack of achievement, with

> "Sense of past Youth, and Manhood come in vain,
> And Genius given, and Knowledge won in vain;
> And all which I had culled in wood-walks wild,
> And all which patient toil had reared, and all,
> Commune with thee had opened out—but flowers
> Strewed on my corse, and borne upon my bier
> In the same coffin, for the self-same grave!"

A bitter foretaste of what he was to feel on that January night nearly three years later was in Coleridge's mouth as he tried to read *The Prelude* this Sunday night in the *Speedwell*, and he could not go on with it. His mind wandered to the contrast with his own lack of achievement on the scale of Wordsworth's, to the paralysis of his will, and what had caused it. His imagination was as active as ever, always storing up new images and illustrations, but the willpower to combine and use the treasures of his storehouse was lacking. Something had diseased it, the same influence which disorganized his health and turned his sleep into "a pandemonium of all the shames and miseries of the past Life from early childhood all huddled together, and bronzed with one stormy Light of Terror and Self-torture". The thought of it was so horrible that he broke into a prayer for strength to do without his fatal stimulant, to amend his life, to live in truth. He abased himself, he pleaded his mitigating virtues, he acknowledged his feebleness, he implored mercy. It is as though you were looking at one of those half-melted faces with a circular hole for a mouth that scream silently at you in a picture by Francis Bacon.

"Sunday Midnight, May 13th 1804" he wrote at the end of his prayer. He was in his bunk by then, though he did not feel like sleeping. There was a noise on deck overhead, and as Captain Findlay came down at the end of his watch, Mrs Ireland asked him what was happening. Captain Findlay's answer carried Coleridge's mood to a nadir of dreariness. "They are setting the mainsail" Findlay said. "It is almost calm again".

Before Coleridge went to sleep he said one more prayer, which was not for himself. He asked for a blessing on Wordsworth, his wife, his sister, his child, on Sara Hutchinson, on his own children, and last on his wife; but after her name he could not help adding "tho' we have lived in Bitterness!"

XXVIII· *Monday 14th May to Thursday 17th May*

The near calm which halted the convoy at midnight on Sunday lasted only a few minutes. The wind revived and blew steadily from the north all night. This was a relief for the Commodore, as the convoy was now nearing the narrow straits between Sicily and Tunis, where the danger of pirates and privateers was again great. Twice in the next two days he signalled the convoy to close up into a more easily defended formation, and the appearance of any strange sails on the horizon was anxiously noted in the *Maidstone*'s log.

The fair wind blew all Monday, but sank to a light breeze as the sun set among fiery clouds shaped like a ruined and blazing city of domes and pillars, which faded to green and then to black as the sky darkened, and the moon and stars glimmered through the thin clouds blown up by the wind as it freshened again. All through Tuesday it blew the convoy onwards; the island of Pantellaria was not far off on their right, and the coast of Sicily should have been visible on their left, but a haze on the horizon hid it. The convoy was making good progress, and expected to be in sight of Malta by noon on Wednesday; but at four o'clock on Wednesday morning the wind shifted to a chilly sirocco from the east. At noon next day the convoy had hardly moved for twenty-four hours, and was dawdling in variable breezes with Mount Etna dimly visible to the north-east.

To Coleridge Thursday was a "delicious day". He was now feeling unusually well, with a good appetite and a feeling of lightness such as he had not had for months. He had stopped dosing himself, and felt alert and wakeful all day, instead of the stupefying drowsiness which had hung over him for so long. The day of sirocco had had a passing effect, giving him a sore throat, a slight temperature, and some aches and pains, and he seized on this as evidence of his peculiar susceptibility to weather, and resolved to keep a journal in Malta to show how his health reacted to changes in wind and humidity. His reaction to the sirocco is in fact common to everyone on their first arrival in the Malta region, and is no evidence for Coleridge's theory about his health; but he had now pushed away again the recognition, which had come into the open in the torturing prayers of a few nights earlier, that it was opium which was wrecking his health. An external cause such as weather was a more bearable way of accounting for his sufferings. His spirits revived, the more so as the end of his voyage was now almost in sight.

He noted in his journal with some surprise that though he was disappointed at the slight delay in their arrival caused by the change of wind, he was not anxiously impatient about it. No one was awaiting him in Malta whom he was longing to see, he thought of his stay there only as a halt on his way to Sicily. He was going to stay in Malta with an old acquaintance, Dr John Stoddart, Advocate at the Admiralty Court in Malta. Coleridge had known Stoddart for four years, though not very well. He thought of Stoddart as an honest, kind-hearted well-informed man, though not a brilliant one.

Stoddart knew Walter Scott, Mackintosh, Godwin and Lamb; he was an author and translator as well as a lawyer. He had warmly invited Coleridge to visit him in Malta, where he had gone the year before with a newly married wife, and Coleridge had reason to expect the kind of welcome—cheerful but not emotional—that would suit him best from an old but not close friend. Disillusion would follow later, when Stoddart proved on nearer acquaintance to be a man of commonplace and unimaginative mind, argumentative, conventional, difficult over money, and hard-hearted to servants and beggars.

Stoddart's household included his sister Sarah, who was later to marry Hazlitt. She was a lively clever sincere woman, but insensitive, inconsiderate and abrupt, and Coleridge from the start was to be offended by her manners and her tedious gossip over trivialities and misfortunes. The hard brassy shine of Sarah Stoddart's temperament could not suit difficult subtle men like Coleridge and Hazlitt, but for personalities with tolerance but low vitality, like Charles and Mary Lamb, Sarah's resilience and glee were life-enhancing. Lamb said that she was one of the few people who are not in the way when they stay with you, and Mary Lamb was her devoted friend, though there was no blindness in her devotion. "I love you for the good that is in you, and look for no change" she said.

When Coleridge was just about to leave for Malta, Mary Lamb wrote to Sarah Stoddart urging her to look after him when he arrived. She said that Coleridge was very ill, and she dreaded the thought of his long voyage. No doubt when he arrived he would "talk and talk, and be universally admired", but he would need looking after, and she begged Sarah and her sister-in-law to be kind affectionate nurses to him, and "behave to him as you would to me, or to Charles, if he came sick and unhappy to you". She envied Sarah the pleasure that Coleridge's unexpected arrival would bring. She and Charles had been indulging in dreams of following Coleridge if he could "get my brother some little snug place of a thousand a year" in Malta.

The joke was a courageous one, as the Lambs were cruelly hard up that spring, Charles having just lost the newspaper work that had supplemented his meagre salary from the East India House. Mary declared that in spite of this they were both in good health and spirits, but Coleridge when he was in London that spring had found Lamb unwell and low-spirited. Coleridge was now truly and trustingly devoted to both the Lambs. Next to Wordsworth, he had said only two months ago, Lamb and Southey were the two men whom he loved best in the world. He was just as fond of Mary Lamb, whom he called his "Heart's Sister". She could always control him when he was over-excited, and comfort him when he was wretched.

The two much-beloved figures—the spindly tippling witty man and the square quiet hospitable woman—stand there so cosily in the affections of all their friends that one can scarcely see the raging flame which arched over them. Everyone loved and trusted Mary Lamb, "the only thoroughly reasonable woman I have ever met" said Hazlitt, "one of the most amiable and admirable of Creatures" said Crabb Robinson; Barry Cornwall paid tribute to her "clear and gentle good sense", Coleridge said she was as dear to him as an only sister. Her letters to Dorothy Wordsworth and Sarah Stoddart are sensible and warm-hearted, wise and balanced.

To me she is a figure of absolute horror, and I would not have had the courage to stay alone in a room with her for a moment. This wise loving reasonable woman seized a knife and killed her own mother. She did it in an access of madness; as soon as she recovered, she imposed on all the world her version of this ghastly event, in which not only was she absolved of all guilt, because not responsible for her actions, but fully justified by a sort of vision that her mother had appeared to assure her that it was a "dispensation of Providence for good", and to shower down blessings on her. The legend that her mother had never really appreciated her, had been unjust to her merits and had tried her beyond endurance, began to spread; Charles Lamb himself, who knew the less definite truth, helped to propagate the legend, perhaps because it comforted and absolved his living sister and could not now harm his dead mother. So tranquil did the comforting conviction of essential innocence make Mary Lamb that many of her friends believed she was quite unaware of what she had done. In her sane periods she was perfectly placid and sweet, and moreover formidably intelligent, with a penetrating insight into the psychology of other people, which gave her a power which she certainly enjoyed.

But almost every year a moment would come when she gave an ominous smile, and then began to grow agitated and violent, and a few hours later she would be back in the madhouse. Were none of them afraid, when they saw that dreadful smile, that what she had done once, she might do again? Probably Charles Lamb himself was afraid, though he never admitted it; he loved his sister so well that he was prepared to run all risks, even that one, to keep her free and at home. But when she told him that she felt an attack coming on, he owned that he was "irritable and wretched with fear", and he was desperately anxious to stop anything—too much excitement or strong feeling, too much silence—which might make her worse. The wonder is, not that Lamb often drank too much, but that he was able to carry on a normal life at all, living with a most beloved sister who, whenever they went on holiday, herself packed a straitjacket in their luggage, to be used if one of her attacks came on.

Coleridge had seen it happening a year earlier. He had seen that terrible smile on her face, had heard her telling her brother with much agony that she felt an attack was imminent, had felt her clutching hands on his own arm and heard her wild talk, and had taken her back to the madhouse himself. He was not frightened of her, but he was fascinated by the weird dichotomy of her personality. During the voyage between Gibraltar and Malta, he jotted down a query which had come to him as he watched the turtle hunt. "The apparent *divisibility* of *Life* in the Turtle etc., metaphysically what does it import?" At some later date he wrote against this entry "Mary Lamb's Friendship". Something in the appealing oddity of the hawk's-bill turtles as they lay on their backs on the *Speedwell*'s deck—square, ungainly, sighing and beating their breasts with their flippers—and something in their rapid plunge into the depths when they eluded their captors, suggested this surprising analogy. Mary Lamb was a short square woman with a gruff voice, who generally had a layer of snuff on her upper lip and a large mob cap on her head. The wisdom and insight behind her homely appearance, and the depths of horror and misery below the wisdom and insight, were a metaphysical mystery; how could such different selves inhabit the same being, living side by side but utterly divided? The question was not academic for a man whose own dreams were haunted by a loathed and terrifying second self. There were more meanings than one in Coleridge's recognition of Mary Lamb as his "Heart's Sister".

XXIX· *Friday 18th May*

On Friday morning the convoy was in sight of Malta. By the early afternoon they were near enough for the *Maidstone* to signal her code number, 414, to the signal tower which gave permission for the convoy to enter the harbour. The ships moved in, past the huge cliffs of fortifications, into the harbour, big as a lake, big enough to hold the whole British Navy, it seemed to Coleridge, and with an amphitheatre of creamy freestone buildings rising all round, and reminding him of Bath, but whiter, steeper, and more strange, with its vast massy ramparts and narrow canyons of streets. The harbour rang with the jangle of bells and the sudden deafening shouts of boatmen and fruit-sellers, bellowing up an ascending scale like a bursting bomb of noise. At four o'clock the *Speedwell* came to rest in the harbour and dropped her anchor.

Coleridge's summary of his frame of mind as he arrived in Malta, was "I am tranquil and resigned—and even if I should not bring back Health, I shall at least bring back experience". He had set out in hope, he arrived in resignation.

There are no simple turning-points in the lives of men like Coleridge. His voyage to Malta was not in vain in the sense that his life, hitherto a success, became a failure, as a man and as a writer, then or later. Even the voyage itself, and the two years in the Mediterranean that followed, were not a dead loss for his later life and work. Ideas for later writings, and for revisions of earlier ones, were garnered during the voyage and in his later travels in Sicily and Italy, and while he was in Malta he got through a lot of bureaucratic business, as Secretary to the Governor, which was a useful mental exercise. He was afterwards to say that his work for the Governor, Alexander Ball, had been in some ways the most instructive part of his life, that he had acquired much useful knowledge of how the machinery of government worked and how to manipulate it. He did "at least bring back experience". In the years after his return to England he wrote all his greatest prose, and profoundly influenced religious and aesthetic ideas in nineteenth-century England, and it was his political and philosophical essays and lectures that he cited in *Biographia Literaria* as the justification of his existence, a life, as he said, not lived in vain. He justly demanded to be judged by what he had achieved, not by what he might have achieved. He challenged the proudest of his literary contemporaries "to compare proofs with me, of usefulness in the excitement of reflection, and the diffusion of original or forgotten, yet necessary and important truths and knowledge".

What made it a voyage in vain was that he did not recapture the ideal self which he had set out to find, and he realized that now he never would recapture it. The ideal of a good and happy life which he had set before himself as a young man, and which still seemed possible when he set out on the voyage to Malta, had dissolved almost to nothing by the time he arrived. He was never going to be one of the great company, to which he had aspired and to which Wordsworth belonged, of the single-minded poets whose total dedication was rewarded by the true good life. He was a different kind of man from what he had supposed himself to be.

It was not that he had never felt despair before he started on the voyage, or that he never felt hope again afterwards. Years before he went to Malta, he had experienced crises of dejection about his poetic powers, and had felt in himself and announced to his friends that he had mistaken his vocation, he was not meant to be a poet; and for years afterwards he was to have occasional quickenings and throbs in the pulse of his hope, and to believe that he might yet become a "regenerated Creature".

But it was in this year of 1804 that he became aware of a change in himself. He had not found what he set out to find, and he no longer really believed that it was findable. He had already recognized the loss of joy, now he admitted the possibility of living without hope. In his more histrionic moments in Malta he sometimes had longings for death, even "whispers of Suicide, toys of desperation". But his more constant mood was a haunting consciousness of change, of growing old, of a narrowing of his heart. On the first night of the voyage, he had a brief visitation of strange misgivings, morbid yearnings to concentrate his being into stoniness. Twelve months later he admitted to himself that 1804 had been the year in which the wide sympathies of his youth had petrified; "then comes the grave-stone into the Heart".

Some years later he was talking with friends about the process of growing old, and someone said that there was a moment in the lives of most men between thirty-five and forty-five in which "a man finds himself at the *Top of the Hill*—and having attained perhaps what he wishes begins to ask himself—What is all this for?—begins to feel the *vanity* of his pursuits—becomes half-melancholy, gives in to wild dissipation, or self-regardless Drinking—and some not content with these—not slow—poisons, destroy themselves". This observation struck cold to Coleridge's heart, because it described so accurately his own experience, his "Sense of past Youth, and Manhood come in vain". "I had *felt* the Truth; but never saw it before clearly; it came upon me at Malta, under the melancholy dreadful feeling of finding myself to be *Man*, by a distinct division from Boyhood, Youth, '*Young Man*'. Dreadful was the feeling—before that, life had flown on so that I had always been *a Boy*, as it were—and this sensation had blended in all my conduct".

What happened to Coleridge in 1804 can be represented as a liberation. When you abandon an impossible ideal, you are more free to concentrate on nearer, achievable, aims. Some of his biographers have suggested that it was a late growing-up at last into real maturity. On this theory Coleridge's pursuit of his first ideal was not a failure but a false start; the author of *The Friend* and *Bio-graphia Literaria* and the Shakespeare lectures had more to give to his fellow-men than the author of *The Ancient Mariner*. After beckoning hope, and vanishing hope, hope with a new face—the real one.

But this is to ignore the extent to which Coleridge remained, still and always, a self-deceiver, and more than ever chained to a deadly habit. The loss of hope can produce endurance and strength; it can also produce paralysis. One can watch Coleridge as he loses hope, and as he realizes that it is irretrievably lost—that he will never be the man that he aspired to be—but there are no scales in which to weigh what was lost against what was gained. He was different, that is all one can say—"utterly changed", as Dorothy Wordsworth wretchedly exclaimed when she first saw him after his return to England. Wordsworth described the difference in a painful poem, at once affectionate and egoistic.

> "There is a change—and I am poor.
> Your love hath been, not long ago,
> A fountain at my fond heart's door,
> Whose only business was to flow;
> And flow it did: not taking heed
> Of its own bounty, or my need.
>
> What happy moments did I count!
> Blest was I then all bliss above!
> Now, for that consecrated fount
> Of murmuring, sparkling, living love,
> What have I? shall I dare to tell?
> A comfortless and hidden well".

There are some lines in Petrarch's *Epistles* which meant a great deal to Coleridge, and which he quoted often in his later writings. He linked them with the passing of love and with the failure of poetic inspiration; with the realization that he was no longer living outside time, as a young man seems to himself to do; that the dawn light would never again project onto his cloudy imagination a a glory round his own head. Petrarch's words are the best expression of what happened to him on this voyage, whose spiritual destination was not the one for which he set out. These are the lines from Petrarch:

"With age all things are gradually consumed, and in living we die and are snatched away while we are still here. In that passing I shall not seem myself: another brow, other habits, a new form of the mind, another voice sounding".

List of Sources

List of Sources

Note: (i) Biographies, memoirs, critical studies and general works are listed under their subject, not under their author, thus—
COLERIDGE, SAMUEL TAYLOR.
House, Humphry. *Coleridge.* Rupert Hart-Davis, 1969,
but with a cross-reference to the author of the work, thus—
House, H. see under COLERIDGE, S. T.
(ii) all titles mentioned were published in London unless otherwise stated.

Adair, P. M. see under COLERIDGE, S. T.
Allsop, T. see under COLERIDGE, S. T.
Anthony, K. see under LAMB, C. AND M.
Bate, W. J. see under COLERIDGE, S. T.
BEAUMONT, Sir George.
Greaves, Margaret. *Regency Patron: Sir George Beaumont.* Methuen, 1966.
Beer, J. B. see under COLERIDGE, S. T.
Berger, Miss. see under TOBIN, J. AND J.
Birrell, A. see under STODDART, S.
Blunden, E. see under COLERIDGE, S. T.
Bodkin, M. see under COLERIDGE, S. T.
Brewster, D. see under COLERIDGE, S. T.
Campbell, J. D. see under COLERIDGE, S. T.
Chambers, E. K. see under COLERIDGE, S. T.
Clowes, W. L. see under NELSON
Coburn, K. see under COLERIDGE, S. T., and HUTCHINSON, S.

List of Sources

COLERIDGE, Hartley.
> *Letters of Hartley Coleridge.* ed. G. E. and E. L. Griggs, Oxford University Press, 1936.

COLERIDGE, Samuel Taylor.
> Notebooks 9 and 15. British Museum Add. MS. 47,506 and 47,512.

Anima Poetae. ed. E. H. Coleridge, Heinemann, 1895.

Biographia Literaria. ed. George Watson, Dent, 1956.

Complete Poetical Works. 2 vols, ed. E. H. Coleridge, Clarendon Press, Oxford, 1964.

Friend, The. 2 vols, ed. B. E. Rooke, Routledge & Kegan Paul, 1969.

Inquiring Spirit: A New Presentation of Coleridge from his Published and Unpublished Writings. ed. Kathleen Coburn, Routledge & Kegan Paul, 1951.

Letters of Samuel Taylor Coleridge. 4 vols, ed. E. L. Griggs, Clarendon Press, Oxford, 1956 and 1959.

Notebooks of Samuel Taylor Coleridge. 4 vols, ed. Kathleen Coburn, Routledge & Kegan Paul, 1957 and 1962.

Table Talk. 2 vols, ed. H. N. Coleridge, John Murray, 1835.

Adair, Patricia. *The Waking Dream: a Study of Coleridge's Poetry.* Edward Arnold, 1967.

Allsop, T. *Letters, Conversations and Recollections of S. T. Coleridge.* F. Farrer, 1864.

Bate, W. J. *Coleridge.* Weidenfeld & Nicolson, 1968.

Beer, J. B. *Coleridge the Visionary.* Chatto & Windus, 1959.

Blunden, Edmund, and Griggs, E. L., (ed.) *Coleridge: Studies by Several Hands.* Constable, 1934.

Bodkin, Maud. *Archetypal Patterns in Poetry.* Oxford University Press, 1948.

Brewster, Sir David. *Letters on Natural Magic.* John Murray, 1834.

Campbell, J. Dykes. *Samuel Taylor Coleridge: a Narrative.* Macmillan, 1894.

Chambers, E. K. *Samuel Taylor Coleridge, a Biographical Study*. Clarendon Press, Oxford, 1938.

De Quincey, Thomas. *Recollections of the English Lake Poets*. ed. J. E. Jordan, Dent, 1961.

Empson, William, and Pirie, D. Introduction to *Coleridge's Verse, a Selection*. Faber & Faber, 1972.

Fruman, Norman. *Coleridge, the Damaged Archangel*. Allen & Unwin, 1972.

Gillman, James. *Life of S. T. Coleridge*. Pickering, 1838.

Grigson, Geoffrey. *The Romantics*. Routledge & Kegan Paul, 1942.

　　　　　The Harp of Aeolus. Routledge & Kegan Paul, 1948.

Hanson, Laurence. *The Life of S. T. Coleridge, The Early Years*. Allen & Unwin, 1938.

Haygarth, John. "Description of a Glory" in *Memoirs of the Literary and Philosophical Society of Manchester*, vol. iii, pp. 463–7, 1790.

House, Humphry. *Coleridge. The Clark Lectures 1951–2*. Rupert Hart-Davis, 1969.

Lowes, J. L. *The Road to Xanadu*. Houghton Mifflin, Boston, 1927.

Margoliouth, H. M. *Wordsworth and Coleridge 1795–1834*. Oxford University Press, 1953.

Minnaert, M. G. J. *Light and Colour in the Open Air*. Bell, 1959.

Potter, Stephen. *Coleridge and S. T. C.* Cape, 1938.

Richards, I. A. *Coleridge on Imagination*. Kegan Paul, 1934.

Sultana, Donald. *Samuel Taylor Coleridge in Malta and Italy*. Blackwell, Oxford, 1969.

Suther, Marshall. *The Dark Night of Samuel Taylor Coleridge*. Columbia University Press, New York, 1960.

Yarlott, Geoffrey. *Coleridge and the Abyssinian Maid*. Methuen, 1967.

COLERIDGE, Sarah (wife of S. T. Coleridge).

Minnow Among Tritons: Mrs S. T. Coleridge's Letters to Thomas Poole. ed. Stephen Potter, Nonesuch Press, 1934.

M

COLERIDGE, Sara (daughter of S. T. Coleridge).
Memoir and Letters. ed. by her Daughter, King, 1873.

Griggs, E. L. *Coleridge Fille: a Biography of Sara Coleridge.*
Oxford University Press, 1940.
Cornwall, Barry. see under LAMB, C. AND M.
DAVY, Humphry.
Davy, John. *Memoirs of the Life of Sir Humphry Davy.* 2 vols,
Longmans, 1836.
Paris, J. A. *Life of Sir Humphry Davy.* 2 vols, Colburn and
Bentley, 1831.
Trenner, Anne. *The Mercurial Chemist: a Life of Sir Humphry
Davy.* Methuen, 1963.
De Quincey, T. see under COLERIDGE, S. T.
De Selincourt, E. see under WORDSWORTH, D. and
WORDSWORTH, W.
ELLIOT, Admiral Sir George.
*Memoir of Admiral the Honble Sir George Elliot. Written for
His Children.* Privately Printed, 1891.
FARINGTON, Joseph.
The Farington Diary. 8 vols, ed. J. Greig, Hutchinson, 1923.
Fruman, N. see under COLERIDGE, S. T.
Gilchrist, Mrs. see under LAMB, C. AND M.
Gillman, J. see under COLERIDGE, S. T.
GODWIN, William.
Paul, C. Kegan. *William Godwin: his Friends and Con-
temporaries.* 2 vols, King, 1867.
Greaves, M. see under BEAUMONT, G.
Griggs, E. L. see under COLERIDGE, H., COLERIDGE,
S. T., and COLERIDGE, Sara.
Grigson, Geoffrey. see under COLERIDGE, S. T.
Hanson, L. see under COLERIDGE, S. T.
Haygarth, John. see under COLERIDGE, S. T.
House, H. see under COLERIDGE, S. T.

HUTCHINSON, Sara.
   Letters of Sara Hutchinson, 1800–1835. ed. Kathleen Coburn,
   Routledge & Kegan Paul, 1954.

Raysor, T. M. "Coleridge and 'Asra' " in *Studies in Philology.*
   vol. xxvi, pp. 305–324, 1929.
Whalley, G. *Coleridge and Sara Hutchinson and the Asra
   Poems.* Routledge & Kegan Paul, 1955.
Kennedy, L. see under NELSON
LAMB, Charles and Mary.
   Letters of Charles and Mary Lamb. 3 vols, ed. E. V. Lucas,
   Dent and Methuen, 1935.

Anthony, Katharine. *The Lambs.* Hammond, 1948.
Cornwall, Barry. *Charles Lamb: a Memoir.* Moxon, 1866.
Gilchrist, Mrs. *Mary Lamb.* W. H. Allen, 1883.
Lucas, E. V. *Life of Charles Lamb.* 2 vols, Methuen, 1921.
Robinson, H. Crabb. *Correspondence with the Wordsworth
   Circle.* 2 vols, ed. Edith Morley, Clarendon Press, Oxford,
   1927.
                    On Books and their Writers. 3 vols, ed.
   Edith Morley, Dent, 1938.
Talfourd, T. N. *Memoirs of Charles Lamb.* Gibbings, 1892.
LEIBNIZ, G. W.
   *Theodicy: Essays on the Goodness of God, the Freedom of Man
   and the Origin of Evil.* ed. Austin Farrer, trans. E. M.
   Huggard, Routledge & Kegan Paul, 1951.
Litchfield, R. B. see under WEDGWOOD, T.
Lowes, J. L. see under COLERIDGE, S. T.
Lucas, E. V. see under LAMB, C. AND M.
MACKINTOSH, James.
   Memoirs of the Life of Sir James Mackintosh. 2 vols, ed. R. J.
   Mackintosh, Moxon, 1836.
Maclean, C. M. see under STODDART, Sarah
Mahan, A. T. see under NELSON
Margoliouth, H. M. see under COLERIDGE, S. T.

Marshall, J. see under NELSON
Minnaert, M. G. J. see under COLERIDGE, S. T.
Moorman, M. see under WORDSWORTH, W.
Naish, G. P. B. see under NELSON
NAVAL RECORDS
 Log of H.M.S. Leviathan 28th March–11th May 1804. Public Record Office ADM. 51/1486.
 Log of H.M.S. Maidstone 20th April–25th May 1804. Public Record Office ADM. 51/1517.
 Muster of H.M.S. Maidstone, 25th April 1804. Public Record Office ADM. 36/15587.
 Regulations and Instructions to His Majesty's Service at Sea, 25th January 1806. Library of National Maritime Museum, Greenwich.
 Signal Book for the Ships of War, 1799. Library of National Maritime Museum, Greenwich.
NELSON, Lord.
 Dispatches and Letters. 7 vols, ed. Sir N. H. Nicolas, Colburn, 1845 and 1846.
 Letters of Lord Nelson to Lady Hamilton, 2 vols, Lovewell, 1814.

Clowes, W. L. *The Royal Navy: a History from the Earliest Times to the Present.* Sampson Low, Marston, 1900.
Kennedy, Ludovic. *Nelson's Band of Brothers.* Odhams, 1951.
Mahan, Captain A. T. *Life of Nelson.* Sampson Low, Marston, 1899.
Marshall, John. *Royal Naval Biography.* 8 vols, Longman, 1823.
Naish, G. P. B. *H.M.S. Victory.* Pitkin, 1972.
Oman, Carola. *Nelson.* Hodder & Stoughton, 1948.
Warner, Oliver. *A Portrait of Lord Nelson.* Chatto & Windus, 1958.
   Nelson and the Age of Fighting Sail. Cassell, 1963.
   H.M.S. Victory: Official Guide and Short History. Portsmouth, 1972.
Oman, C. see under NELSON

List of Sources

Paris, J. A. see under DAVY, H.
Paul, C. K. see under GODWIN, W.
POOLE, Thomas.
Sandford, Mrs Henry. *Thomas Poole and His Friends*. 2 vols, Macmillan, 1888.
Potter, S. see under COLERIDGE, S. T., and COLERIDGE, Sarah
Raysor, T. M. see under HUTCHINSON, S.
Richards, I. A. see under COLERIDGE, S. T.
RICKMAN, John.
Williams, Orlo. *Lamb's Friend the Census-Taker: Life and Letters of John Rickman*. Constable, 1912.
Robinson, H. Crabb. see under LAMB, C. AND M.
Sandford, Mrs H. see under POOLE, T.
Simmons, J. see under SOUTHEY, R.
SOUTHEY, Robert.
Life and Correspondence of Robert Southey. 6 vols, ed. C. C. Southey, Longmans, 1850.
New Letters of Robert Southey. 2 vols, ed. Kenneth Curry, Columbia University Press, New York, 1965.
Selections from the Letters of Robert Southey. 4 vols, ed. J. W. Warter, Longmans, 1856.

Simmons, Jack. *Southey*. Collins, 1945.
STODDART, Sarah.
Birrell, Augustine. *William Hazlitt*. Macmillan, 1902.
Maclean, C. M. *Born Under Saturn: a Biography of William Hazlitt*. Collins, 1943.
Sultana, D. see under COLERIDGE, S. T.
Suther, M. see under COLERIDGE, S. T.
Talfourd, T. N. see under LAMB, C. AND M.
TOBIN, James and John.
Berger, Miss. *Memoirs of Mr John Tobin*. Longmans, 1820.
Trenner, A. see under DAVY, H.
Warner, O. see under NELSON

181

List of Sources

WEDGWOOD, Tom.

Litchfield, R. B. *Tom Wedgwood, The First Photographer.* Duckworth, 1903.

Whalley, G. see under HUTCHINSON, S.

Williams, O. see under RICKMAN, J.

WOOLF, Virginia.

A Writer's Diary. Hogarth Press, 1965.

WORDSWORTH, Dorothy.

Journals. 2 vols, ed. Ernest de Selincourt, Macmillan, 1941.

---

de Selincourt, Ernest. *Dorothy Wordsworth.* Oxford University Press, 1933.

WORDSWORTH, John.

Letters of John Wordsworth. ed. C. H. Ketcham. Cornell University Press, Ithaca, 1969.

WORDSWORTH, Mary.

Letters of Mary Wordsworth, 1800–1855. ed. Mary Burton, Clarendon Press, Oxford, 1958.

WORDSWORTH, William.

Poetical Works. 5 vols, ed. E. de Selincourt and Helen Darbishire, Clarendon Press, Oxford, 1946–1952.

The Prelude, or the Growth of a Poet's Mind. ed. E. de Selincourt, revised Helen Darbishire, Clarendon Press, Oxford, 1959.

Letters of William and Dorothy Wordsworth, ed. E. de Selincourt,

I. The Early Years 1787–1805, revised C. L. Shever.

II. The Middle Years 1806–1811, revised Mary Moorman. Clarendon Press, Oxford, 1967 and 1969.

Memorials of Coleorton: Being Letters from Coleridge, Wordsworth and His Sister, Southey and Sir Walter Scott to Sir George and Lady Beaumont, 1803–1804. 2 vols, ed. W. Knight, D. Douglas, Edinburgh, 1887.

Moorman, Mary. *William Wordsworth: the Later Years.* Clarendon Press, Oxford, 1965.

Yarlott, G. see under COLERIDGE, S. T.

Index

Index

Index

Index